"Read this book and be strengthened. Yo ███ an amazing amount of wisdom for the Ch ███ tors!). Surprising, even striking, sentences ███ good at putting people down, except on his ▂▂▂▂▂ ▂▂▂▂▂▂ ▂▂▂▂▂▂▂ ▂▂▂ church through the observing and writing of Don Carson."

—MARK DEVER, Senior Pastor, Capitol Hill Baptist Church, Washington, DC

"In a day when we honor megachurch pastors, it is refreshing to read this account of an ordinary pastor—representing the unsung heroes among us who do not aspire to greatness but rather to godliness and faithfulness. This account of Dr. Don Carson's father gives us valuable insight into the life of a man who accepted the challenges of ministry with both integrity and grace, and in the telling of his story we are also treated to a rare insight into the life of a Protestant pastor in French Québec. This book is a powerful reminder that there are no little places if we are faithful to the God who called us. Read it to be blessed, challenged, and instructed in matters that really count."

—ERWIN W. LUTZER, Pastor Emeritus, Moody Church, Chicago

"*Memoirs of an Ordinary Pastor: The Life and Ministry of Tom Carson* is a deeply edifying and timely book. Faithfulness, not numbers, not 'success,' not novelty, not 'relevance,' but faithfulness is the accrediting mark of gospel ministry, and that message comes through loud and clear from introduction to conclusion of this memoir. Reading it brought to mind the powerful words of Anna Waring: 'content to fill a little space, if Thou be glorified.' I found the content profoundly evocative and pastorally instructive. In a day and age of celebrity preachers and personality-driven ministries, it is utterly refreshing to be instructed and encouraged by the recounting of unfamous, lifelong, biblical fidelity in gospel labors. Read. Repent. Be encouraged. And then go thou and do likewise."

—LIGON DUNCAN, Senior Minister, First Presbyterian Church, Jackson, Mississippi; President, Alliance of Confessing Evangelicals; Adjunct Professor, Reformed Theological Seminary

"This book is a rare and precious gift from one of evangelicalism's greatest scholars. It is rare, because given our modern fascination with megachurches and celebrity pastors, we tend to overlook the simple, faithful pastor. It is precious for ordinary pastors like me, because Tom Carson's life is a biblical and inspiring model for pastoral ministry—ministry that is centered on the gospel, marked by integrity, and faithful to the end. How generous of Dr. Carson to bequeath his father's quiet legacy to us all. May every pastor and Christian who reads this book aspire to pass on such an 'ordinary' legacy."

—C. J. MAHANEY, Senior Pastor, Sovereign Grace Church of Louisville

"How can the application of a Bible-saturated mind (Don's) to a Bible-saturated life (Tom's) produce an even more helpful story to encourage pastors? Let the 'mind' be carried on a river of love because the 'life' is his father's. Then add a kind of narrative creativity you didn't know Don Carson had. That's how."

—JOHN PIPER, Founder, desiringGod.org; Chancellor, Bethlehem College & Seminary

"Scores of books assure us—ordinary us—that we were meant to be extraordinary or to accomplish extraordinary things for God. Well, thank God, this small book by D. A. Carson is not one of them. Recounting part of his father's *ordinary* life and ministry, and reflecting upon it in his characteristic gospel-centered, lucid way, Dr. Carson strikes at the heart of what's wrong with us when we forget that, as servants, we were meant to live ordinarily under the gospel of grace. Read this book. You will be deeply encouraged in your life and ministry. You might also stand corrected about your take on true success. Perhaps you will even end up praying you'll be deemed as ordinary as Tom Carson was."

> —MICHEL LEMAIRE, Pastor of Église Baptiste de la Foi,
> Drummondville, 1984-2005

"Those of us ministering in French Canada are proud to point out that D. A. Carson got his start among us here in Québec. In *Memoirs of an Ordinary Pastor,* not only do we get an intimate glimpse of that start, through the life and times of his father and mother, but we also get another facet, another perspective, of the rich history of the Fellowship Baptist movement in Québec. Obedient and faithful men, like Tom Carson, laid the foundation so others could build upon it. Ordinary builders working on an extraordinary building, the dwelling place of God in French-speaking living stones. *Gloire à Dieu!*"

> —REV. TERRY CUTHBERT, Fellowship French Region
> Church Planting Director; Former President, FEBCC

"Here is D. A. Carson's most personal book, providing us with details about his early years in French Canada. This story about his father, documented from Thomas Carson's personal journals, correspondence, and posthumous testimonies, is a clear demonstration of God's faithfulness toward a man whose integrity, patience, and deep commitment to French Canadians brought eternal results amidst little fruit, poverty, discouragement. In our twenty-first-century tendency toward glamor, our obsession with numerical growth, and expectancy for quick results, this personal testimony is a healthy reminder of heavenly priorities in the pastorate and Christian ministry."

> —PIERRE CONSTANT, Associate pastor, Église Baptiste
> Montclair de Hull, 1982-1997; Professor of
> New Testament Studies, Toronto Baptist Seminary

MEMOIRS OF AN ORDINARY PASTOR

The Life and Reflections of Tom Carson

D. A. CARSON

:: CROSSWAY®

WHEATON, ILLINOIS

ISBN-13: 978-1-4335-0199-9
ISBN-10: 1-4335-0199-6
ePub ISBN: 978-1-4335-2210-9
PDF ISBN: 978-1-4335-0312-2
Mobipocket ISBN: 978-1-4335-0688-8

Library of Congress Cataloging-in-Publication Data
Carson, D. A.
   Memoirs of an ordinary pastor : the life and reflections of
Tom Carson / D. A. Carson.
     p. cm.
   ISBN 978-1-4335-0199-9 (tpb)
   1. Carson, Tom, 1911– 2. Baptists—Canada—Clergy—
Biography.
I. Title.
BX6495.C38C37   2008
286.092—dc22   2007042374

Crossway is a publishing ministry of Good News Publishers.

CH   27 26 25 24 23 22 21 20 19 18 17

Thomas Donald McMillan Carson
26 August 1911—26 October 1992

Elizabeth Margaret Maybury Carson
6 January 1909—31 December 1989
In memoriam

CONTENTS

PREFACE

*S*ome pastors, mightily endowed by God, are remarkable gifts to the church. They love their people, they handle Scripture well, they see many conversions, their ministries span generations, they understand their culture yet refuse to be domesticated by it, they are theologically robust and personally disciplined. I do not need to provide you with a list of names: you know some of these people, and you have been encouraged and challenged by them, as I have. Some of them, of course, carry enormous burdens that watching Christians do not readily see. Nevertheless, when we ourselves are not being tempted by the green-eyed monster, we thank God for such Christian leaders from the past and pray for the current ones.

Most of us, however, serve in more modest patches. Most pastors will not regularly preach to thousands, let alone tens of thousands. They will not write influential books, they will not supervise large staffs, and they will never see more than modest growth. They will plug away at their care for the aged, at their visitation, at their counseling, at their Bible studies and preaching. Some will work with so little support that they will prepare their own bulletins. They cannot possibly discern whether the constraints of their own sphere of service owe more to the specific challenges of the local situation or to their own shortcomings. Once in a while they will cast a wistful eye on "successful" ministries. Many of them will attend the conferences sponsored by the revered masters and come away with a slightly discordant combination of, on the one hand, gratitude and encouragement and, on the other, jealousy, feelings of inadequacy, and guilt.

Most of us—let us be frank—are ordinary pastors.

Dad was one of them. This little book is a modest attempt to let the voice and ministry of one ordinary pastor be heard, for such servants have much to teach us.

Sporadically across a ministry that spanned almost six decades, Dad kept journals. There is almost nothing from the first twenty-five years (roughly 1933–1959); most of the journals belong to 1959–1992. Yet these latter documents sometimes comment with perceptive retrospection on Dad's memories of the early years. Even in the years covered by the journals, Dad sometimes went for a block of time without recording anything. At other times he recorded nothing more than the mundane details of his ordinary ministry: his sermon preparation, lists of people he visited that day, mundane duties of administration, his prayer lists, picking up the kids from school—that sort of thing. And sometimes he carried on for pages of self-reflection, confession, addressing God through his words on the page in heart-wrenching intercession. Certainly he never expected any of his lines to be published: he wrote as a matter of self-discipline, to hold himself accountable. He was not trying to write classic devotional literature.

In addition to his journal, he penned thousands of pages of sermon notes. Ever the pack rat, he kept all the letters he received, and copies of many of the letters he wrote. After Dad had left this life, my brother Jim sent me all the files, and I found every letter I had ever sent home—two or three thousand pages. And clippings: Dad kept envelopes and files and scrapbooks of clippings from newspapers and other publications, trying to keep abreast of what was going on, not only in his own patch but, selectively, throughout the world.

At one point I wondered if there was enough worthy material in the journals to make a book. In that case, these "memoirs of an ordinary pastor" would have been using the word *memoirs* in the sense that the plural form usually enjoys: the work would have been autobiographical, and I would have merely edited it. You would have had before you Dad's "take" on his ordinary ministry. But frankly, the journals as a whole do not lend themselves to publication. Large chunks of his life and service would not have been accounted for—and in any case, countless pages do not merit wide circulation. So eventually I decided to make this book an amalgam. I have tried to weave together some of the material in Dad's journals ("memoirs" in the narrow sense) with memories and reports from other people (what a "memoir" often refers to in the singular). My brother and sister have sent along several pages of their own memories and reflections; the churches Dad served have loaned me their records; trusted friends in Québec have advised me what books and essays I should read to remind myself of the time and place when and where Dad served.

Sometimes I have appealed to his letters, especially in the early years of his ministry when he was not keeping a journal. Where I have done so, I have usually masked the names of those who wrote or those who received letters from Dad by using their initials, for some of these folk are still alive, and certainly most of their children are. Occasionally I have edited these materials in order to correct obvious mistakes (typos and the like), but I have taken care not to change the meaning. When I have inserted an asterisk beside the date, it is to indicate that I have not included everything Dad wrote for that date, but only part of it.

So this is not a critical biography. If it were, I would have included much more about Dad's ancestry, far more factual details of his ministry, a full account of his wife and our Mum, prolonged probing of the social and historical circumstances of his life and service, more theological probing of his thought, and an attempt at a critical evaluation of his life. But my aim is much more modest: to convey enough of his ministry and his own thought that ordinary ministers are encouraged, not least by the thought that the God of Augustine, Calvin, Spurgeon, and Piper is no less the God of Tom Carson, and of you and me.

Three more brief explanations will set the stage. First, the bulk of Dad's ministry was in French Canada. That is a foreign culture to many readers in the English-speaking world; so in the first chapter I've tried to fill in at least a few of the details needed to make Dad's vision and passion coherent. In the first half of the twentieth century, Québec was the most Roman Catholic "nation" in the world, if that can be assessed by the per capita numbers of priests and nuns it sent out as Catholic missionaries to other countries. Evangelical witness was extraordinarily difficult. Between 1950 and 1952, Baptist ministers spent a total of eight years in jail for preaching the gospel (though the charge was inevitably something like "inciting to riot" or "disturbing the peace"). By contrast, today Québec is astonishingly secular, even anti-clerical. Dad's life spanned the years of dramatic change—though rarely at the time did Dad or other ministers fully grasp the significance of the changes through which they were living.

Second, Dad's journals were written sometimes in English, sometimes in French. English prevails in the early years of the journals; the final years are mostly in French. Sometimes Dad would switch from one language to the other in the middle of a sentence, or back and forth several times in the middle of the day's entry. Here, of course, everything has been put into English. Beginning his ministry when he did, inevitably his English Bible was the King James Version; his French Bible was the less outdated Louis Segond Version of 1910. Neither is widely used today, but in deference to Dad's historical and cultural location, I've preserved the KJV for Dad's Bible quotations, unless he himself departs from the older versions. I have, of course, translated the rare snippets of Greek, Hebrew, and Latin.

Third, I have decided to refer to Dad as Tom (as all his friends called him) in the ordinary course of this book, and to Mum (that's the dominant Canadian spelling where British influence prevails) as Marg or Margaret (Dad often called her "my dear" but commonly addressed her or referred to her as Marg; he sometimes wrote of her as Margaret). The exception will be when I am talking about family matters. Then they will become "Dad" and "Mum" again.

My thanks to my sister Joyce and my brother Jim for their anecdotes, suggestions, and criticisms. Heartfelt appreciation goes to Michel Lemaire for providing me with important materials that I would have had to spend a lot more time gathering myself. It would be unthinkable to finish this Preface without expressing gratitude beyond measure to Église Baptiste de Montclair and its two pastors during the final years of Dad's life, viz. the brothers André and Pierre Constant. I know full well that these men and many others feel indebted to Dad. All I can say is that they and the church they served discharged the debt full well in the love and support they provided him during Mum's eight-year descent through Alzheimer's and in his final three years of living on his own. For you see, he was never on his own. God displayed his great love for him in the church's faithful care, making sure the chores around the house got done, even encouraging him in his return to preaching, visiting, and counseling again, at the age of seventy-eight.

At the risk of saying too much prematurely, I end this Preface with two observations. The first is that Dad's "glass half-empty" awareness of his failures and inadequacies rarely aligns with the view of him taken by his contemporaries. I've given this discrepancy a lot of thought and will reflect on it from time to time in this book. The discrepancy may say something important to other ordinary pastors who are feeling discouraged. Second, few assessments of Dad's journals are likely to prove more penetrating than that of Michael Thate, my administrative assistant. Michael cheerfully transcribed the English parts of the journals. When he sent me the last digital files, he accompanied them with an e-mail that said in part, "I used to aspire to be the next Henry Martyn [heroic British Bible translator and missionary to the Muslim peoples of India and Persia]. However, after reading your dad's diaries, the Lord has given my heart a far loftier goal: simply to be faithful. I know we as men are but dust, but what dust the man I read about in these diaries was!" And after proofing the manuscript he sent me a note telling me he was reminded of Tolkien's lines about Strider:

> All that is gold does not glitter,
> Not all those who wander are lost;
> The old that is strong does not wither,
> Deep roots are not reached by the frost.
> From the ashes a fire shall be woken,
> A light from the shadows shall spring;
> Renewed shall be blade that was broken,
> The crownless again shall be king.

All true. And yet Tom was a most ordinary pastor.

D. A. Carson
Trinity Evangelical Divinity School
Soli Deo gloria

O CANADA!
A SKETCH OF QUÉBEC

*E*very life and every ministry have a historical context. When that context is very similar to that of the reader, very little needs to be said about it. Tom's context was quite different from that of most people who will read this book. Since he cannot readily be understood apart from that context, this short chapter supplies what is needed.

Canada

The first Europeans to settle the country we now call Canada were French. Jacques Cartier arrived in 1535—many decades before the Pilgrim Fathers landed several hundred miles farther south. Many of the French settlers were trappers and fur traders—*coureurs de bois*, they were called, literally "runners of the woods." They established linked communities and trading posts at strategic points along the St. Lawrence River, down through the Great Lakes, across to the Mississippi River, and down the Mississippi to New Orleans. They thus encircled what became the Thirteen Colonies, whose residents tended to be more agrarian.

The differences between the French and English settlers were more than economic and geographic. The French were solidly Catholic and brought French traditions of churchmanship, education, and government with them. The American settlers were mostly from England, a mix of Congregationalists, Anglicans, and Presbyterians, and eventually Baptists and Methodists. Inevitably the perennial European conflicts between France and England spilled over into the new world. Even within French Canada—then called New France—tensions in Europe generated violence. In France the Edict of Nantes had guaranteed remarkable religious freedom for the fast-growing Protestants, the Huguenots. In 1685, however, King Louis XIV of France revoked the Edict of Nantes. Tens of thousands of Huguenots were killed or sent to the galleys or simply fled. Historians continue to debate how many of them were put to death in New France.

Meanwhile, rising numbers of English-speaking settlers were making their homes to the east of Québec in Acadia. It was not until the British took over New France that substantial numbers of such settlers made homes for themselves further inland, in what was later called Ontario. The turning point came in 1759. General Wolfe from England led a flotilla of warships up the St. Lawrence to Québec City, the seat of government for Québec, pondering how to land his troops and lead them up the sharp escarpment without being slaughtered by the massed French troops on the heights. In the dead of night, he managed to get them up a tiny trail that was left unguarded, and in the morning there was a classic battle on the Plains of Abraham, just outside the city itself. The English won. Both General Wolfe and the defending French General Montcalm were killed. The English took over governance of New France, and this arrangement was finalized and enshrined in the Treaty of Paris, signed at Versailles on 10 February 1763, between France and England. Canada and the American States were ruled from London. By 1791 a distinction was made between Lower Canada and Upper Canada. Lower Canada—so-called because it was situated on the downstream parts of the St. Lawrence, the area we now call the Province of Québec—was French-speaking and Roman Catholic, and its influence stretched through the Great Lakes and down the Mississippi to New Orleans. Upper Canada—so-called because it lay upstream on the St. Lawrence system, in what is now Ontario—was traditionally English and Protestant.

In 1776, when the American War of Independence broke out, not all Americans were convinced that rebellion against the British crown was the right thing to do. Thousands of Americans trekked north and resettled in Upper and Lower Canada. In Canada they were known as UELs—United Empire Loyalists. Historians have sometimes compared the sermons of American patriots in this period with the sermons of UELs: how was the Bible handled in the two populations? Yet not only was there a deep rift between UELs and other Americans, there was also a fundamental division among the UELs themselves. Those who arrived in Upper Canada were absorbed by a population that spoke English and was largely Protestant; those who arrived in Lower Canada faced a thoroughly alien world. Some small percentage of them founded new communities that spoke, taught, and worshiped in English, forming little villages with names like Sawyerville—English Protestant enclaves that were largely left to themselves. But most UELs who settled in Lower Canada eventually intermarried with the French population and were absorbed into its culture and religion. That is why it is still possible to visit towns that are virtually 100 percent French-speaking and find significant numbers of families in the phone book with names like Williams, Smith, and Rogers who cannot understand a word of English.

Subsequent events in American history were sometimes mightily influenced by these developments in the neighbor to the north. Two are worth mentioning. Ongoing tensions between England and America were equally tensions between Canada and the United States, surfacing most dramatically in the War of 1812–14. At the beginning of the nineteenth century, Britain was at war with France, struggling to defeat Napoleon, and used its navy to impede American trade with France, which, understandably, America viewed as illegal restriction of free international commerce. The Royal Navy also pressed many Americans into its service. Equally frustrating to the Americans was the British strengthening of the French-Canadian and Indian forts around the Great Lakes and down the Mississippi to New Orleans, arming them with a ready supply of the most up-to-date weapons. The Americans were now trying to move west and viewed these military developments with alarm. On 18 June 1812 the Americans declared war on Britain and invaded Canada.

The struggle does not need to be reviewed here: it is the outcome that is important to our story. Americans viewed the conflict as a second war of independence, while the British were less interested in this conflict than in the war with France. Once Napoleon was defeated, that war had achieved its primary aim. Britain cut its losses and signed the Treaty of Ghent on December 24, 1814 to end the war with America. Before news of this signing could reach the U.S. southern coast, United States forces won a resounding victory at New Orleans (its losses on land had been considerable up to that point, including the sacking of Washington and failure to take any part of Canada), while British forces captured Fort Bowyer in Alabama. Canadian and American history books read the results in very different ways. Seeing this (as I've said) as a second war of independence, Americans not only saw the outcome as a resounding victory (the Battle of New Orleans is the stuff of legend) but also found themselves more united as a nation than they had been before the war.

Proud and grateful that they had lost none of their territory, Canadians also saw the outcome as a resounding victory, for under the capable leadership of General Sir Isaac Brock they had successfully repulsed invading American forces, and they too found themselves more united than before the war. Many in the francophone population did not particularly like the British government, but they certainly preferred it to the American, for they feared they would be swamped by America's English language and culture, not to say its Protestantism, if they fell under rule from Washington. Residents of Upper and Lower Canada began to think of themselves as having a good deal more in common with each other than with their neighbors to the south. That newly born sense of unity ultimately resulted in the founding of Canada.

The second major event that must be understood is the birth of Canada. It was not until 1867 that the Dominion of Canada was born under the terms of the British North America Act (now called the Constitution Act, 1867). Until that time Canada (called British

North America until 1867) was essentially ruled by governors sent out from Britain's Parliament at Westminster. Now Canada secured full legislative freedom, barring the right to change the Constitution independently, a right not repatriated (as it was called) to Canada's House of Commons until 1982. The reason for this delay was not that Westminster was begrudging about giving up its power; rather, Canadians could not agree on a formula for changing their own Constitution. Until 1982 changes were made (akin to constitutional "Amendments" in the U.S.) through Westminster. The inability to agree sprang in large part from Canada's substantial minority of French-speaking citizens, understandably nervous about potential constitutional amendments that would take away their unique rights. These we must understand if we are to grasp the shape of evangelical ministry in Québec in the mid-twentieth century.

Québec

Just as the fledgling United States kept adding states until it reached its current total of fifty, so fledgling Canada kept adding provinces until it reached its current total of ten, plus three territories. The last province to be added was Newfoundland (1949). From its beginning, however, Canada had to agree to establish a constitution that would ensure that the provinces enjoyed certain legal rights that would allow Québec to preserve its peculiar linguistic, cultural, and religious character. Although there is a minority of French Canadians in Ontario, along with tiny pockets in Alberta and about a fifty-fifty split in New Brunswick, only Québec enjoys an overwhelming majority of francophones. Although Québec is only one of ten provinces, nevertheless throughout much of the twentieth century about one-third of Canadian citizens claimed French as their first language. (The percentage has in recent years dropped slightly to about 30 percent.) The result was a constitution that made both English and French, at least on paper, official languages of the entire country. Moreover, it granted the provinces enormous legislative rights in virtually every domain except criminal law, national economic policy, and foreign affairs. In other words, although the other nine provinces developed laws that were roughly in line with British heritage, in Québec criminal matters were constrained by laws derived from the British heritage, but civil, religious, educational, and other cultural sectors were constrained by laws adapted from the heritage in France, frequently from the Napoleonic Code. Perhaps the greatest exception was in the area of religion, where Québec followed neither Britain nor France. Québec never went through anything analogous to the French Revolution with its strenuous anti-clericalism. Québec laws granted enormous authority to the Catholic Church, especially in the domain of education.

Until the 1960s and 1970s, the influence of the Catholic Church among the six million or so francophones in Québec is difficult for those who never lived through that time to imagine. An astonishingly high percentage of the population attended weekly Mass, and the will of the Church was mediated through thousands of priests. It is essential to understand at least a little of what this looked like.

First, the birthrate was very high, and the abortion rate was very low. In many parts of Québec, the average number of children per family was eight. The family that lived behind our home had eleven children. Down the road from where we lived was a family with twenty-one children, no multiple births, one mother. This is not hearsay; we knew the family. It was not uncommon to hear priests urging *la revanche des berceaux* ("the revenge of the cradle"): the English may have taken over the country by military might, but the disparity in birthrates would sooner or later renew French and Catholic strength.

Second, the form of Catholicism in Québec at the time was frankly medieval. This was Catholicism still untouched by Vatican II (1962–1965) and largely uninfluenced by European secularization or the Reformation. I remember the indulgences that were sold, the sight of devout pilgrims climbing the stairs of l'Oratoire St-Joseph on their knees while reciting the Rosary at each step, and popular forms of adoration of Mary that I have seen duplicated nowhere in the world except Poland. I recall the vast crowds that turned out to see Cardinal Léger ride slowly in an open car down the main street of our city, and as he passed, everyone—well, everyone except the Carsons—fell to their knees or even flat on their faces before him by the side of the road, a human wave that followed the progress of the car.

Third, the Catholic clergy openly encouraged a certain kind of isolationism from the rest of the country. Some of this was understandable. If too many learned English, perhaps the French language, history, and culture would be obliterated. Nevertheless, the system that produced priests, nuns, and lawyers tended not to produce engineers and senior managers, for they would have to interact with peers who spoke English. The result was inevitable: English Canadians, never slow to push their own interests, tended, even within Québec, to be the managers, the bosses, the planners, at least on the economic fronts, while French Canadians were the laborers. Resentments were festering that would explode into violence in the 1960s. These resentments were also fueled by basic inequities. Nominally both English and French were national languages, but whereas an anglophone could be tried in an English-speaking court in Québec, a francophone could not be tried in a French-speaking court in most of the rest of the country. Road signs in Québec were bilingual; elsewhere in the country, they were only in English. A box of cereal that sold across the country was printed only in English.

The fourth factor was perhaps the most important for Tom's ministry in the early years. The Catholic Church had so much authority, through the Québec legislature, in the domain of education that two school boards were set up—one Catholic and the other Protestant. The so-called Protestant School Board was not really religiously Protestant at all. It more or less paralleled the provincial school boards of the other provinces: essentially it was moving in the direction of increasing secularization. Catholics, Protestants, Jews, and anyone else could attend. The catch was that this Protestant School Board was permitted to have schools in the English language only. By contrast, the Catholic School Board was distinctively Catholic. Often the teachers were nuns and teaching brothers; it was not uncommon for a priest to be in charge. In other words, the public system for six million francophones in Québec was essentially like a conservative Catholic parochial school today. These schools, of course, were mostly French. Here, too, there was a catch. If a French-speaking family with children in the (French) Catholic school system converted and, say, became members of a Baptist church, sometimes they were no longer allowed to send their children to the Catholic system.

Where this happened—it was common enough, though it depended greatly on local administrators—the parents soon discovered that if they wanted to send their children to a school under the Protestant School Board, whether because they were forced to or out of theological conviction, the schools of the Protestant Board were in English. There were no French-language schools under the Protestant School Board. Not only did the children often lose a year learning the English language, but over time their friends became English, and their reading skills and educational strengths were in English, and so when they grew up many of them drifted toward English churches. That meant that the French evangelical churches tended to be perennially first-generation churches, since many of the children defected to the English side.

By the beginning of the twentieth century, there were about seventy French-speaking evangelical Baptist churches dotted up and down the St. Lawrence Valley, most of them belonging to the Grande Ligne Mission. Most of these were small, and some faced the challenges of being perennially first-generation. Theological liberalism wiped out almost all of these churches in the early decades of the twentieth century. By the mid-1930s, only a handful remained, along with a few francophone Plymouth Brethren assemblies, serving a population of six million.

This was the context in which three men—Wilfred Wellington and Tom Carson, both from English-speaking Canada, and a man from Switzerland, William Frey—in the late 1930s committed themselves to full-time church-planting in French Canada. Frey, of course, was fluent in French; the other two had to begin by learning the language. But before we take up that story, it is important to understand how massively Québec has changed in the last seven decades.

Just as many other countries in the Western world went through their own forms of 1960s and 1970s rebellion, so also did Québec. While America smoked pot in Haight-Ashbury, agonized over Viet Nam, and tore itself apart over Watergate, Québec developed its own homegrown terrorists. They called themselves the FLQ, the *Front de libération du Québec*, and thought of themselves as avant-garde Marxist revolutionaries as they detonated about two hundred bombs between 1963 and 1970. Their violence killed five people and seriously wounded scores more. The end came in October 1970 when the FLQ kidnapped British trade consul James Richard Cross (later released) and snuffed out the life of Pierre Laporte, the Vice-Premier and Minister of Labour of Québec, allegedly strangling him with his rosary chain. Encouraged by Jean Drapeau, the Mayor of Montréal, and Robert Bourassa, the Premier of Québec, Prime Minister Pierre Elliott Trudeau invoked the War Measures Act, effectively imposing a form of martial law across Canada. The FLQ was quickly broken (their cells had already been penetrated by anti-terrorist police), and martial law was lifted.

Trudeau was shrewd enough to see that some grievances had to be addressed. In short order not only cereal boxes but anything that was sold across the nation had to use bilingual advertising, and any project that was federally funded—major highways, for instance, and airports—had to deploy bilingual signs. This was initially irritating to Canadians in English sectors of the country, but in reality they were merely facing the flip side of what French-speaking Canadians had experienced for years. Immersion schools were set up across the country for learning the other language, and the court system became more equitable.

As recently as 1972, there were only about forty evangelical French-speaking local churches in Québec, half Baptist and half Plymouth Brethren, all of them small—so small that those who had paid ministers could afford them only because of supporting grants from churches in English Canada.

But Québec was changing. In the eight years from 1972 to 1980, the number of such assemblies and preaching points grew exponentially to almost five hundred, some of them of substantial size, and representing numerous denominations. In some ways this was a singular movement of the Spirit of God. Yet God normally uses means, and hindsight sometimes affords a glimpse of those means. In the providence of God, the way for this growth was paved, in part, by the increasing restlessness of Québec youth, growing awareness of a larger world, and the corresponding weakening of the Catholic Church, especially in the cities. From 1960 on, Québec experienced what came to be called the Quiet Revolution, a rubric covering major pieces of legislation and a wide array of cultural shifts. In September of that year, Jean-Paul Desbiens, a friar and educator, published *Les insolences du frère Untel* ("The Impertinences of Brother So-and-So"), a hilarious satire on the manifold weaknesses of the educational system in Québec and a runaway best-seller. The pressure for change was on.

Though they were merely small pieces in the Quiet Revolution, three educational policies pursued by the Provincial government turned out to have a huge unforeseen impact on the gospel. The first was the determined push for more science and engineering in the universities, combined with the formal end of the Catholic Church's control of education in the Province. The second was the invention, in 1967, of the CEGEP system. CEGEP is a French acronym for *Collège d'enseignement général et professionnel* (College of General and Professional Education). High school ended at year eleven. Students who wanted to go further attended a CEGEP, which offered either a three-year diploma for one of the "skill" or "trade" professions, or a two-year pre-university course before going off to university. In 1967, the year they began, there were twelve CEGEP schools; today there are forty-eight, six of them English-speaking. When the gospel began to make enormous strides from 1972 on, very often it was among the students, especially the young men, of the fledgling CEGEP system. Hundreds of them were soundly converted, and many became, over the next few years, the nucleus of the next generation of French evangelical leaders.

Third, in November 1969 the Québec legislature passed an Act to Promote the French Language in Québec (known as Bill 63). Its purpose and achievement were both complex, but one of the effects of this and other steps in educational reform was that

French-speaking schools could be accessed by anyone regardless of religion; another of its effects was that French was favored in a variety of ways. Thus it became a lot easier to build a second- and third-generation evangelical church.

Today the city of Montréal has the highest per capita number of tertiary (post-high school) students of any city in North America, including Boston. Québec has the highest abortion rate and the lowest birthrate in North America. These latter statistics may not be applauded, but they constitute one measure of the almost embarrassing weakness of current Québec's ancient Catholic heritage. The percentage of Canadians whose mother tongue is French is shrinking slightly, and the primary reason it is not shrinking faster is because of the rising numbers of Haitian immigrants who bring their French and Créole with them. *La revanche des berceaux* ("the revenge of the cradle") is over. Québec is now notoriously secular, except in remote villages—and even there the vitality of the Catholic Church has been sapped.[1] Tom Carson lived through much of this change. In 1972, when the gospel began to advance rapidly, Tom turned sixty-one.

---

[1] Most readers of this volume will probably not be interested in the many technical studies of social and religious change in Canada, and specifically in Québec, in the decades that concern us. For those who may be interested, however, the place to begin is the important essay by Mark A. Noll, "What Happened to Christian Canada?" *Church History* 75 (2006): 245–273. See also Hubert Guindon, "Chronique de l'évolution sociale et politique du Québec depuis 1945," available online at http://classiques.uqac.ca/contemporains/guindon_hubert/chronique_evol_qc/chronique.html. Less reliable is the work of Glenn Smith, "Le mouvement 'évangélique' au Québec depuis 1960," *Revue Scriptura* 7/2 (2005): 29–46, whose figures do not always align very well with those of Statistics Canada. In particular, his analysis of his figures depends upon the flawed (though admittedly popular) definition of "evangelicalism" offered by Bebbington (David W. Bebbington, *Evangelicalism in Modern Britain: A History from the 1730s to the 1830s* [London: Unwin Hyman, 1989], 2–17). The result is that he finds that fewer than 1 percent of Québeckers call themselves "evangelicals" (Statistics Canada, with a slightly different question, puts the figure at 2.7 percent), but about 30 percent of Catholics identify themselves with Bebbington's four defining characteristics of evangelicalism and therefore must be considered evangelical Catholics. In reality, what this analysis displays is the hopeless inadequacy, especially in a Catholic context, of the Bebbington grid.

CHAPTER TWO

TOM CARSON: BEGINNINGS OF LIFE AND MINISTRY

*T*om was born in Carrickfergus, Northern Ireland, on 26 August 1911, to John and Ethel Carson. At the ripe age of two, Tom emigrated with his parents and older brother Reg to Ottawa, Canada's capital city, where his father worked as a printer until he retired. Eight years after the family arrived in Canada, a sister, Maureen, was added. In those days Ottawa was a predominantly English-speaking city, but although it was situated in Ontario, it was right across the Ottawa River from Québec and the almost entirely French-speaking city of Hull (now rechristened Gatineau). Today Ottawa is closer to eighty-twenty anglophone and francophone; Hull remains predominantly French-speaking.

During the years the family was growing up, and throughout the early years of Tom's ministry, his father John was not a Christian. John became a believer a few months before he died, at a time when I, one of his grandchildren, was old enough to observe the difference. But Tom's mother Ethel was a faithful Christian woman who ensured that her children were exposed to the gospel through the ministry of Calvary Baptist Church in Ottawa. Tom became a firm Christian during his high school years. He graduated from Ottawa Collegiate Institute (a high school) in 1927. The grade scheme at the time was very much in the British tradition: grade inflation was unheard of. The highest mark in the class for chemistry was 66; Tom's grade was 59, with the notation "Very fair." In geometry, the highest grade was 87, and Tom got it. In Latin Authors and Latin Composition, the top grade was 167, and Tom earned 149, with the curt notation "Good." French (oral, authors, and composition) earned the same note. Under history, the teacher wrote, "Good. Should succeed. Needs to review."

Both then and later he was much influenced by an elderly Christian man at Calvary to whom he always referred as "old Mr. Blair." Old Mr. Blair devoted himself to the young men at the church, in high school and beyond, grounding them in Bible study and basic doctrine, and stamping them with wisdom gleaned from eight decades of experience. During the years Tom worked in Ottawa for Metropolitan Life, while he was juggling his job, assorted lay ministries in the church, and sports (he won more than one regional swimming championship), he began to wrestle with whether he should give his life to vocational ministry. He complained to old Mr. Blair that "there just isn't enough time." Always suspicious of lame excuses and of anything that even hinted at the suggestion that God could have arranged the disposition of time a little better, old Mr. Blair smiled, put his arm around Tom's shoulders, looked directly at him, and quietly said, "Tom, you have all the time there is." That was all.

Tom went to seminary. The year was 1933, and the Great Depression blanketed Canada as much as the rest of the Western world. Tom attended a small institution called Toronto Baptist Seminary (TBS). Since TBS features crucially in Tom's story a decade and a half later, it is worth taking a moment to understand the school.

Just as at the end of the previous century C. H. Spurgeon faced the "Downgrade Controversy" in England and started his own training institution (known today as Spurgeon's College), and just as J. Gresham Machen split from his Presbyterian denomination and started Westminster Theological Seminary in Philadelphia (Machen's *Christianity and Liberalism* should still be required reading in theological curricula), so Baptists in Canada had their own clash between historic confessionalism and rising liberal theology. The focal point was the divinity faculty of McMaster University in Hamilton, Ontario. On the conservative side was T. T. Shields, the highly influential pastor of Jarvis Street Baptist Church in Toronto.

Tensions had been rising as Shields tried to establish theological accountability at the University. Not only in his preaching but in his radio broadcasts and publications Shields was trying to arouse Baptist constituencies to the theological dangers he perceived. Jarvis Street published a monthly journal called *The Gospel Witness*. As I write these lines, I have in front of me issue 5/26 for 4 November 1926. The lead article, in variously sized fonts, is titled "Ichabod! (I Sam. iv, 21.): McMaster's New Name." The entire 176-page fascicle is given over to verbatim reports from the Baptist Convention of that year, plus analysis of much of what was said.

The issues with which Shields was dealing were not peripheral. For instance, one of the sections of the document to which I've just referred records discussion of the atonement. A Professor Marshall mocks and openly dismisses any notion of penal substitution. "I will not surrender John 3, 16. (Applause.) I will not surrender those glorious words, to me the greatest music of the New Testament: 'God commendeth His love towards us, in that, while we were yet sinners, Christ died for us'" (p. 99). Anyone who has even the slightest sympathy for historical theology understands that penal substitution, rightly understood, glories in the love of God. To argue that the theme of God's love undercuts penal substitution may have scored victories with the ignorant, but it is woefully inept theology. That it carried the day is a terrible testimony to the weakness of Canadian Baptist understanding of elementary theology at the time. Moreover, anyone who has even the slightest sympathy for careful exegesis understands that John 3:16 itself occurs in a context that does not mock the wrath of God but addresses it (see John 3:36). Marshall goes on to talk about "theories of the atonement" and even cites James Denney and Charles Spurgeon to support his position. Shields has no difficulty demonstrating that he has misrepresented both Denney and Spurgeon.

Shields was not certain, in that issue of *The Gospel Witness*, that the struggle was over, but he feared the worst. The next year, 1927, brought the irreconcilable split. Many Baptist churches left the association, and Shields founded Toronto Baptist Seminary. In governance it was under Jarvis Street Baptist Church. It became the training institution for (primarily Baptist) would-be pastors no longer happy to undertake their training at McMaster.

So when Tom began his studies at TBS in 1933, the Seminary was young, exciting, small, and very much part of a movement that felt it was in the vanguard of the defense and promulgation of the gospel. It attracted a remarkable group of students, not a few of whom went on to significant ministry. One of these was Arnold Dallimore, who in time would write the magnificent two-volume biography of *George Whitefield*. He was a year ahead of Tom at the Seminary. Almost sixty years later, shortly after Tom died, Dallimore wrote me. His letter said in part:

> I first met Tom in September, 1933. I had spent the summer in Québec province delivering Gospels in the French tongue from door-to-door. My company was Bill Hall, younger brother of Rev. James Hall, pastor of Calvary Baptist Church, Ottawa.
>
> At the close of the summer, as we were returning to Toronto Baptist Seminary we spent a week-end in Ottawa and arranged to take two young men with us, Ed Hall and Tom Carson who were about to begin their first year at the Seminary. Tom proved a diligent student and he and I became warm friends. During my fourth year at TBS we had adjoining rooms on the third floor of a rooming house and shared a kitchen and a clothes closet. I always enjoyed Tom's company and appreciated his sense of devotion to God.

Another student of those days, Walter Tompkins, who roomed with Tom during part of their Seminary days, wrote about him, "His prayer life is a challenge and rebuke to most of us."

Money was extremely tight. There was no fiscal help from home: Tom's father thought he was making a terrible mistake. On at least one occasion Tom traveled the 280 miles from Toronto to Ottawa for a visit home by riding his bicycle: it took him three days, and he slept in barns along the way. The summer of 1934, after his first year at Seminary, he spent distributing literature door-to-door in Québec, for that was the direction in which he was already looking. His high-school French was still far too fragile for serious ministry, but his partner that summer was Frédéric Buhler from France, who, inevitably, did most of the talking.

In 1937 Tom, still single, agreed to serve Emmanuel Baptist

Church as pastor. Emmanuel was an English-language congregation in Verdun, part of metropolitan Montréal. Tom accepted the invitation with the understanding that he would spend part of his time improving his French, and after a few years he would resign and try to plant a French-speaking church in that city.

The language barrier was critical. Just as many anglophone Canadians outside Québec speak no French, many francophone Canadians within Québec speak no English. Many on both sides are bilingual, of course, but English speakers, whether from Canada or from America or elsewhere, are often surprised to discover how many Canadians do not speak their language or share large parts of their cultural heritage. As recently as a *Time* essay in 1995 (46/20: 48–51), one French-Canadian woman was quoted as saying, "I've never met an English-speaking Canadian. But I'm sure they are as nice as any other foreigner." That is as good a reminder as any that until people born and reared in francophone Québec took up the task of church planting, others who undertook the challenge faced cross-cultural barriers that were not only linguistic but had to do with perceptions of the world, self-identity, sense of history and sense of humor, inherited literature, and countless other factors. Without ever ministering outside his adoptive country of Canada, Tom committed himself wholly to the francophone heritage. In that sense, this little book might as readily be titled *Memoirs of an Ordinary Missionary*. Many years later, when I myself was a pastoral intern under another man, Ernest Keefe, who had devoted himself to French Canada, I was given a vivid lesson in the commitments of some of these early pastors/missionaries. Ernie and I were returning from a long day of visitation in a fairly remote village, all in French, of course, and as we drove along we were chatting in English. After a few minutes Ernie interrupted: "Sorry, Don, but I'm too tired to think in English. If you don't mind, we'll go back to French." Tom Carson traveled that same route toward complete identification with French Canadians.

Tom's years at seminary also witnessed a blossoming romance with Elizabeth Margaret Maybury, who had been a student at TBS ahead of Tom. Marg was born in London, England, and emigrated to Canada with her siblings and widowed mother when Marg was fourteen. More than two years older than Tom, Marg was already a nurse and midwife. In terms of grades at the Seminary, she usually did better than Tom. After her years at TBS she returned to nursing and applied to three different missions, volunteering to serve in Africa. They all turned her down for health reasons: she suffered from chronic anemia. So she agreed to marry Tom. The wedding took place on 28 April 1938, officiated by W. Gordon Brown, a close associate of T. T. Shields, another name that features prominently in the crisis recounted two chapters from now. Since both Tom and Marg had attended Jarvis Street during their years at TBS, they had both enjoyed hearing Shields during his best years.

Jarvis Street Baptist Church and other churches formed The Union of Regular Baptist Churches of Ontario and Québec, and it was this Union that helped support them during the early years of the French work. In Canada, the expression "Regular Baptist" was never associated with dispensational premillennialism as it was in the U.S. They simply saw themselves as "Regular Baptists" as opposed to the new liberal Baptists.

This is not a book that focuses on Mum. Here and there she inevitably comes into the account, of course, but a few comments here will not be inappropriate. Her health problems meant that she often needed to sleep for an hour or two in the afternoon or she simply could not cope. In some ways I was closer to her than to Dad: I certainly spent more time talking with her in private than I did with Dad. She was amazingly insightful on a wide range of both personal and theological issues. My sister Joyce recalls that when she returned home for a visit during her own training to become a nurse, she went out with a friend one evening and then the two returned home to continue conversation. When the friend left (Joyce writes),

> Mom mentioned to me how interested I can appear when the topic is important to me, but how I obviously tuned out my friend when she spoke of things that mattered to her but that I didn't care about. Although I resented her analysis at the time, I soon took a second look at what she said and realized that it was all too true. The memory of those words have helped me greatly over the years when I see myself reverting to this un-Christlike behavior.

When I was in my mid-teens and going through a phase when I wanted to pull away from meetings both local and regional because (I pouted) those who attended didn't have my interests, and they all cared about themselves, and much more of the same, my mother, sitting quietly at her treadle sewing machine (for years she made most of our clothes), quietly quoted two or three proverbs, and then added, "He who would have friends must show himself friendly. At the next meeting, before you go into a sulk, look around for the loneliest person in the room, and go and find out everything you can about that person. Then find the next loneliest person, and do it again." Inevitably I resented the advice, but I took her up on it and to my amazement was soon regarded as one of the region's youth leaders. Mum rarely took up a point like that twice; once we were in our teens, she rarely nagged. But she was always right on target with a piquant way of spelling out the practical implications of doctrines, commandments, and grace. In my mind's eye I see her still, sitting in the kitchen after breakfast with her Bible on her knees, having her own quiet time, or disappearing into her bedroom for the same purpose. Tom was a workmanlike expositor, faithfully committed to explaining the biblical text. Marg's Bible studies (e.g., for our youth groups and the like) were simply superb.

Despite her brightness and insight, the one area she never mastered was spoken French. This severely limited her ability to minister to women and others in the church unless they spoke English—some did, and some didn't. Even in her late sixties she tried to beat this handicap by taking conversational French courses at the local college. But she never really cracked that barrier. At the family level, that meant a good deal more English than French was spoken in the home; at the ministry level, Mum was cut off from many conversations and developments, and this had isolating effects for both her and Dad.

Their first years, however, were in English ministry. Their small flat on Woodland Avenue was their home for their first decade, for they remained there as the French side of Tom's ministry began to grow in the early 1940s. Many ministers of the gospel went as chaplains with the Canadian Forces fighting the war against Hitler.

(Canada actually declared war on Germany a few hours before Britain did!) Tom wrestled with the decision, looked at the healthy ratio of chaplains to foot soldiers, compared the ratio of gospel ministers to the population of Québec, and thought it wiser to stay. Nevertheless, constrained by the national crisis, he did apply for the chaplaincy, but was turned down owing to a heart murmur. Tom could stay in French Canada with a clear conscience.

Emmanuel Baptist in Verdun became the sphere where Tom gained his early experiences of week-by-week pastoral ministry. Few papers from that period of his life remain. His ordination took place on 28 May 1941. Two years later, in 1943, my older sister Joyce was born. By the time I came along in 1946, Dad was already entirely enmeshed in the French work.

The transition to the French side did not take place all at once, but by late 1943 almost all his energies were in the fledgling French ministry. Even as late as 1945, however, Dad was asked to take his turn, with other English-speaking pastors in the Montréal area, to provide several "Morning Meditations" for English radio covering the metropolitan area. He agreed to do this every year until 1948, when the family moved to Drummondville. All the manuscripts survive. By contemporary standards, the language is old-fashioned and stilted, but one must remember that in the English schools of the Protestant Board of Education the Bible was still taught (King James Version, of course), and virtually everyone who prayed did so in Elizabethan English. Canadians were not then biblically illiterate as are most Westerners today. What is interesting about these addresses is not their archaic and sometimes technical terminology, but the mix of commitments they reflect: biblical exposition, personal application, reflection on the national and international scene, a willingness to refer to hymns that just about everyone recognized at the time, and invariably something that challenges, however indirectly, Roman Catholic theology. Here is the full script for 19 April 1945. The original has a scribbled note in pencil in the margin at the top: "2 minutes too long"—and the same pencil has scratched out about two minutes worth of reading. Here is the edited result:

Open

"Not unto us, O LORD, not unto us, but unto thy name give glory, for thy mercy, and for thy truth's sake.

"Wherefore should the heathen say, Where is now their God?

"But our God is in the heavens: he hath done whatsoever he hath pleased.

"Their idols are silver and gold, the work of men's hands. They have mouths, but they speak not: eyes have they, but they see not. They have ears, but they hear not: noses have they, but they smell not. They have hands, but they handle not: neither speak they through their throat.

"They that make them are like unto them: so is everyone that trusteth in them.

"O Israel, trust thou in the LORD: he is their help and their shield. O house of Aaron, trust in the LORD: he is their help and their shield. Ye that fear the LORD, trust in the LORD: he is their help and their shield.

"The LORD hath been mindful of us: he will bless us; he will bless the house of Israel; he will bless the house of Aaron. He will bless them that fear the LORD, both small and great."

Prayer

We come into Thy very presence boldly and with full assurance, O Lord, through Thy well-beloved Son. We thank Thee that He has cleared the way; that when we were yet enemies in our minds by wicked works, when we were without strength and ungodly, Christ died for us.

Thou hast told us that He came into the world to save sinners, to seek and to save that which is lost. Therefore, we pray that Thou mayest enter into some abject and defeated soul to-day to give that wondrous liberty wherewith Christ makes free.

We thank Thee for the encouraging progress of the war. Thou hast been mindful of us. O, continue with us. Yet, Lord, there are many, many thousands of broken hearts and broken-down bodies as the result of this awful turmoil. O Thou Who art called the God of all comfort, let not such suffering ones turn away from Thee; may rather they seek Thee through thy dear Son, and finding Thee, find rest.

Be with our King and Queen; be with our nation; uphold the great nation to the south of us. Establish thou thy peace in many hearts, that those called upon to discuss the question of security in the forthcoming conference may do so with an eye single to Thy glory, through Him Who is alone the Prince of peace, the Lord Jesus Christ. In His name we ask these things. Amen.

Rock of ages, cleft for me.
Let me hide myself in Thee;
Let the water and the blood
From thy riven side which flow'd,
Be of sin the double cure:
Save me from its guilt and power.

Not the labour of my hands
Can fulfil thy law's demands;
Could my zeal no respite know,
Could my tears forever flow,
All for sin could not atone;
Thou must save, and Thou alone.

Nothing in my hand I bring;
Simply to thy cross I cling.
Naked, come to Thee for dress;
Helpless, look to Thee for grace.
Foul, I to the fountain fly;
Wash me Saviour, or I die.

While I draw this fleeting breath,
When mine eyes shall close in death,
When I soar to worlds unknown,
See thee on Thy judgment throne;
Rock of Ages, cleft for me,
Let me hide myself in Thee.

On these mornings in which I am privileged to address you, I shall try to direct your thoughts to the brief consideration of three eternal verities, namely, The Eternal Saviour, The Eternal Word of God, and The Eternal Life of every true child of God. This morning, then, our meditation will be upon "The Eternal Saviour".

The second stanza of that great and well-known hymn, "Abide with me", portrays the earnest desire of one who gazes upon the disappearing landmarks of life to place his feet on an unchanging foundation, and to be upheld by a changeless hand:

Swift to its close ebbs out life's little day;
Earth's joys grow dim, its glories pass away;
Change and decay in all around I see;
O Thou Who changest not, abide with me.

The poet has the firm conviction that *thus* being laid hold upon and cared for would make him a partaker of the nature of this unchanging Friend. Who is this Friend? What is His ministry? On behalf of whom does He exercise this ministry?

You will find in the epistle to the Hebrews, chapter seven, some verses which give us an answer to these questions. The writer is contrasting the superiority of the priestly ministry of the Lord Jesus with that of the priests of the law, and he continues, "And they truly were many priests, because they were not suffered to continue by reason of death. But this man, because he continueth ever, hath an unchangeable priesthood. Wherefore he is able also to save them to the uttermost that come unto God by him, seeing he ever liveth to make intercession for them."

(1) *Who, then, is this Friend?* It is Jesus, the Living One: "He ever liveth." The words "He ever liveth" suggest His identity. He is God manifest in the flesh. The mystery of the Incarnation is a mystery still; but once we lay hold upon that transcendent truth, doubt as to the power of our living Lord to help—nay, to save—will vanish. Indeed in this same epistle to the Hebrews He is first of all introduced to us as the Sovereign Lord: "God . . . hath in these last days spoken unto us by his Son . . . and, 'Unto the Son he saith, Thy throne, O God, is forever and ever' and again, '*Thou, Lord*, in the beginning hast laid the foundation of the earth; and the heavens are the works of *thy* hands. They shall perish; but *thou remainest*; and they all shall wax old as doth a garment; and as a vesture shalt thou fold them up, and they shall be changed: but *thou* art the same, and *thy* years shall not fail." There is no doubt therefore as to His ability to do something for us. *He can save to the uttermost.* He is the Living One. "He *ever liveth*."

But "when all around my soul gives way" is He willing to be "all my hope and stay"?

(2) Well, consider His ministry: "He ever liveth to make intercession." Jesus Christ is the mediator between God and men. And we *need* Him who is "holy, harmless, undefiled, separate from sinners" to intercede for us, for "*God is light*, and in him is no darkness at all".

Eternal Light! Eternal Light!
How pure the soul must be,
When, placed within Thy searching sight,
It shrinks not, but with calm delight
Can live, and look on Thee.

O how shall I, whose native sphere
Is dark, whose mind is dim,
Before the Ineffable appear,
And on my naked spirit bear
The uncreated beam?

There is a way for man to rise
To that sublime abode—
An offering and a sacrifice,
A Holy Spirit's energies,
An Advocate with God.

"An Advocate with God"—my Friend. Jesus ever liveth "to make intercession". But how shall he plead *our* cause? We have already sinned and come short of God's glory. Our very righteousnesses in His searching eye are but as filthy rags. How shall he plead for us?

Five bleeding wounds He bears,
Received on Calvary;
They pour effectual prayers,
They strongly plead for me:
"Forgive him! oh, forgive," they cry,
"Nor let that ransomed sinner die."

"He ever liveth to make intercession", and He has Himself made reconciliation by His blood. It is no wonder that He urgently and lovingly says to you and to me, "Come unto me, all ye that are weary and heavy laden, and I will give you rest."

This very invitation fittingly introduces us to the third question:

(3) For whom does He exercise this ministry of intercession? "He ever liveth to make intercession *for them that come unto God by Him.*"

It is not a choice between the Lord Jesus and other mediators. It is a choice between the Lord Jesus and none at all. God tells us in His word, "There is one God, and one mediator between God and men, the man Christ Jesus." The Lord Jesus Himself said, "I am the way, the truth, and the life: no man cometh unto the Father but by me." Of those alone who come unto God by *Him* is it said, "He is able also to save them to the uttermost." God's message is this:

The soul that on Jesus hath leaned for repose
I will not—I will not—desert to its foes;
That soul, though all hell should endeavour to shake
I'll never—no never—no never forsake.

We need no less than this living, all-powerful Saviour. And He is all we need. For "He that spared not his own son, but delivered him up for us all, how shall He not with him also freely give us all things?"

CHAPTER THREE

FRENCH WORK IN MONTRÉAL

*T*om's initial focus in working among the 85 percent of the people in Montréal whose mother tongue was French was to offer free French New Testaments. Most Catholic families did not in those days possess any part of the Bible. Through the Union that supported him Tom printed thousands of little blue slips offering the New Testament for free: one simply had to write to an address and ask. Sometimes these slips were dropped off in mailboxes, door-to-door; sometimes they were left in prominent places to be picked up. At one time radio spots were used. Anyone who wrote in and asked for a copy of the New Testament received one in the mail. Initially these were mailed from Toronto, later from Montréal. Tom usually followed up these mailings by further correspondence and a visit. Montréal is a spread-out city, and in those days Tom had no car. He resorted to public transport and bicycle. This was Tom's way of trying to get Bible studies going. When the lists of people to follow up became too long, he kept in touch with those who had received a New Testament by sending pamphlets and other literature, along with letters, sometimes handwritten, sometimes typed.

Many letters written to him during this period survive. Some are the initial requests for a copy of the New Testament. Many others tell him not to contact them anymore, whether in person or in correspondence. Tom answered all of these personally, acceding to their request, but often with a final appeal to read certain passages from the Bible or the like.

Opposition of various kinds was growing. One letter, dated 17 June 1945, reads in part:

Dear Pastor,

Several days ago I asked my wife why the Pastor had abruptly stopped visiting us. She replied in an angry voice that you had indeed come to the door, but that she had not let you in and had given you back [a book you had given us]. Then she blew up in a violent scene over my prospective change of religion, warning me that if I converted that would be the end of the marriage.

So I must apologize to you for this strange and incomprehensible attitude my wife has adopted. If I am to have peace, you will understand that I am obligated to bend to her will. I will always be grateful to you for the several hours of instruction you kindly gave me. . . .

As compensation for the pains you have taken I am enclosing a check for ten dollars. This was all that my wife would permit me to give, but I hope to send the same amount secretly in about two weeks. You certainly deserve it.

I close, Pastor, with all the respect owed you, asking the Lord that he may give you strength and courage for the mission with which you have been charged, however ungratefully it is received, as it brings glory to our Lord Jesus Christ.

L.B.

In the context of the theological climate of the time, as people began reading their Bibles points of tension inevitably revolved around an array of issues that chipped away at the exclusive sufficiency of Christ. Are human priests truly mediators between God and sinful human beings, or is Christ the only mediator? Should we pray to Mary as the Mother of God and the one who is most likely to hear our prayers with compassion, or should we address Jesus directly? Is our confidence that our sins are forgiven grounded in the absolution granted by priests, an absolution that turns on such things as the confessional and the Mass, or on the promises of the gospel? Is it possible to secure "grace" by substantial gifts and good deeds that earn "indulgences," or is saving grace grounded exclusively on the finished work of Christ on behalf of his people? It is probably difficult for Western Christians in today's world to grasp how deeply divisive it was, within the closed community of French Canada at that time, to challenge the common assumptions of the Catholic community. Few people came to experience the liberty of the gospel without passing through turmoil. The challenge faced by those early evangelical pastors in Québec was how to confront misconceptions faithfully so that the good news could be seen for what it is, without being unnecessarily confrontational. How does one make people feel the sheer weight of the issues without appearing merely to want to win an argument?

A pair of letters to Tom dated 9 January 1947, written in semi-literate French, illustrate the perennial challenge of the day. Here is the first:

> I am writing to tell you to no longer send anything to me because we pay little attention to your gospeling. . . . Your letters will not stop us from seeing our priests. You don't amount to anything in comparison with the church. You are only capable of sending out letters. . . . You know that our priests are more elevated than you people are and you will never be able to weaken them because this is the true religion and besides I am enclosing examples [i.e., torn-up bits of Tom's letters] to show you what we do with your letters, and if I ever run into my cousin M. [who apparently had asked Tom to write to this family] I assure you I'll tear a strip off her.
>
> One who believes in the Church and its priesthood and in the true Catholic religion,
>
> *Miss M.M.*

Enclosed in the same envelope was a letter along the same lines from the mother, Mrs. M. This note said much the same thing, and even some of the same expressions were picked up. It also included the sentences, "A time will come when you will have need of a priest

and you won't have one. You are all a band of young people who
don't know anything in a conspiracy together."

It was always a challenge to know how to respond courte-
ously yet firmly while helping people to see that eternal issues were
involved, and at the same time respectfully shutting down the correspondence as they requested. In this case Tom replied a little more
forcefully than he usually did:

15 January 1947
Dear Mrs. and Miss M.,

I have received your letters of 9 January advising me
that you no longer wish to receive our literature.
We shall respect your request, and you will receive
nothing further.

Apparently you have not found it helpful to read
the Gospels by Saint Matthew, Saint Mark, Saint Luke,
Saint John, the Acts of the Apostles, and all the
writings of the apostles Saint Paul, Saint Peter,
and Saint John, together with the letters of Saint
Jude and Saint James, all of which are contained in
the book often called simply "The Gospel" or "The New
Testament." [Tom is here using terminology that would
have been coherent to the Catholics of the day. Virtually no one would have referred to, say, "Matthew";
it had to be "Saint Matthew."]

Our sole goal is to persuade people to test by this
Gospel book the statements of those who claim to me-
diate the Word of God to us—rather than to test the
words of our Lord Jesus Christ and of his apostles
by the words of others, whether of your priests or
of us. As for ourselves, gospel Christians, we have
nothing to fear from such a test.

This step you are unwilling to take. On the last
day, it will not be our words or our pamphlets that
will judge you. Jesus himself has said, "Whoever re-
jects me and does not receive *my words* has what will
condemn him: the word that I have spoken, this is
what will condemn you on the last day." (The Gospel
of Saint John, chapter 12, verse 48)

May God give you grace and open your eyes before it
is too late. For understand this: the only Saviour is
Jesus. He wants your whole heart without reserve. May

the peace of the Lord Jesus, who shed his precious
blood to grant this peace, be truly on you.

Your devoted friend,
T. D. M. Carson, Pastor

Opposition was not only personal: in some instances the police were getting involved. In a letter written on 28 February 1944, and sent to Rev. H. C. Slade (who dispensed from Jarvis Street Church the Union funds that supported Tom's work), Tom wrote in part:

As mentioned in a former letter, Mr. Jubinville [a
recent convert] is quite aggressive [in evangelism].
Last Monday afternoon he and I went from door to door
on one of the streets adjoining the church where we
hold our Sunday evening service. We had been visiting for about an hour and a half when a police car
drove up. They called to me and asked if we had a
permit for distributing our circulars. I told them
that they were purely religious circulars, that I
was a Baptist minister, and that I did not know that
I needed to have any special authorization. I showed
them a copy of one of the tracts we were distributing, "The Best Priest in the World." He told us to
stop and that we could not distribute such without
a permit. I asked him where we should get this. He
told us from the Police Department. I thought that
it was best to make further inquiries before doing
anything. . . . [They] asked if the other man—Mr.
Jubinville was on the other side of the street—was
working with me. I said "Yes." So . . . they stopped
their car a little farther on [where he was], and
told him also to desist. Mr. J. offered them a tract
and gave them a big smile.
    On Friday I went to seek a permit. . . . They did
not issue them at the ordinary License Bureau. I
went over to the Bureau of Licenses in the Police
Department. The clerk there told the Lieutenant what
I wanted, but the Lieutenant would not handle it:
"Better see the head of the Department, Captain L."
After visiting for a little while in the vicinity, I
returned to see the Captain. He read the tract and,
not knowing what to do, went into another room—I supposed to see a higher authority. After about ten minutes he emerged and said, in effect, "Well, as far as

I know there is nothing to stop you from distributing
these things without a license or a permit. However,
you had better write to the Chief of Police, as I
should not like to say so on my own authority." He
was quite friendly, and when the business was concluded he asked me concerning what I believed, and I
had some opportunity to give him the gospel. However
I discovered that he was not at heart interested in
my preaching. Nevertheless, he was friendly. On leaving I went to see the Chief. . . . [He] informed me
that there was no permit required, and that we may go
ahead and distribute the tracts. I reminded him that
we had already been stopped. He said that if anyone tried to stop us . . . [we] should send them to
the Police Department. I would like to have this in
writing, but it is some help just the same. I really
had to laugh to myself at all the fuss that was made
because an insignificant Baptist minister was visiting to distribute some religious tracts. . . . When I
was talking with the Captain at the first, after he
had come back from seeing someone higher up, he said,
"Are you a Jehovah's Witness?" I replied, "Decidedly
not, but even if I were, would I not have the right
to distribute religious tracts door-to-door since
the ban has been lifted?" He admitted that he thought
that I would. Well, that is the first small round
with the authorities. There may be more to follow.

There was indeed more to follow.

One of the interesting features of this letter, however, is Tom's
defense of the right of Jehovah's Witnesses to distribute literature.
This was a typical move for him: once he had thought through a
matter of principle, he took a stand on that principle unflinchingly.
Several years later, when persecution was more systematic and ministers were going to jail, there was a rather celebrated court case in
Montréal against some Jehovah's Witnesses. A great deal of public
opinion had been stirred up against them. Tom wrote to the editorial
page of *The Montréal Star* supporting the constitutional right of the
Witnesses to freedom of religion. Tom had worked out the separa-
tion of church and state to his own satisfaction, and he saw that
however much he disliked the theology of the Witnesses, defense of
their freedom was part and parcel of the defense of freedom of all

religious persons. His letter was picked up by the national press and printed across the country. A while later Tom received a letter from the Witnesses' lawyer thanking him for writing. He commented that Tom's was the only letter of support he received from the general public.

These years saw small but measurable encouragements. There is a steadiness and zest in Tom's correspondence for the period. In turn, a stack of letters written to him testifies to the gratitude that many felt for the free New Testaments. Sometimes a contact would ask Tom to read a book in return. One such book was *Le livre d'or des âmes au purgatoire* (i.e., *The Golden Book of the Souls in Purgatory*). Tom read the book and thereby enjoyed yet another topic that spawned fruitful discussions about the gospel.

One man who started reading first the New Testament and then the entire Bible was Charlemagne St-Onge. He was contacted by door-to-door visitation but was already being influenced by local Jehovah's Witnesses. Eventually he asked both Tom and the Witnesses to come to his home and talk out in front of him their respective understandings of what the Bible teaches, allowing him to ask questions. At the end of the marathon meeting, Charlemagne St-Onge decided that what Tom was teaching was better grounded in Scripture than what the Witnesses were saying. He asked the latter never to return, and in due course he and his wife trusted Christ wholly and were baptized in early 1943. Charlemagne St-Onge and his wife bore witness to her brother. He too was converted, and that brother was Mr. Jubinville, who within months was visiting door-to-door with Tom. The very afternoon they were stopped by the police, Mr. Jubinville had collected the names and addresses of six people who requested that free New Testaments be sent to them.

The St-Onge home soon became one of several centers for weekly meetings, in their case every Sunday afternoon. A handful of other adults and children were attracted to the meeting. Some of the connections developed from the unsung ministry of two remarkable women, Miss Bush and Miss Courtney, sponsored by CSSM (the Canadian Sunday School Mission). These two women would hire English-language schools for after-school youth clubs but run the clubs in French (no French school, all of them under the Catholic School Board, would rent space to them). At some schools they had as many as two hundred kids attending—including the St-Onge children, who attended the club in the Alexandra school. So did a child from the Lafrance family. That family was drawn to the meetings in the St-Onge home, and soon the Lafrance home became another center. The St-Onge children, reasonably bilingual, attended an English-language Vacation Bible School at the Earl Gray school in the summer of 1943 and met another child by the name of Jean Hamelin. Through them he heard of the meetings in their home, and because his mother tongue was French he started attending there on Sunday afternoons. In due course he too was converted, and he and one of the St-Onge children were baptized in 1945, using the facilities of an English-language congregation, Snowdon Baptist Church. Another Bible study was started in the Hamelin home.

I recently met with Jean Hamelin, along with one of the St-Onge children (Jacques) and one of the Lafrance children (Michelle), all of them now comfortably senior citizens. They were full of stories of those early years. Somewhere Tom obtained a film of the life of Jesus and was showing it when the police confiscated it. Tom commented to his little flock that he hoped it would do the police a lot of good. It was eventually returned. The St-Onge children were permitted to continue at their local French Catholic school, but eventually tensions ran high enough that the other children were told that if they talked to the St-Onge kids during the school day they would be penalized with detentions. The sanctions were duly imposed but eventually petered out. On one occasion the St-Onge family learned that neighborhood kids were planning on pelting Tom with tomatoes, eggs, and rotten fruit when he came out of the Sunday afternoon meeting in their home. They begged him to leave the back way. Tom replied that he had entered by the front door and he would leave by the front door. Somehow the neighborhood kids got the time wrong, and no one was there to oppose Tom when he left. Inevitably the St-Onge children saw this as another example of God's watchful kindness over this small flock. When the neighbor-

hood kids showed up half an hour late, it took a lot of persuading
to convince them that Tom Carson had already left the building.

Those Sunday afternoon meetings devoted time to the children
as well as to the adults. In a letter to a supporter written in 1944,
Tom wrote:

> Mr. Jubinville and Mrs. St-Onge, brother and sister
> . . . with their wife and husband respectively, seem
> to be making real progress in the way of the Lord.
> Following the marriage of their young brother a week
> ago last Saturday, they were at the reception. It had
> been hard for them to find an opportunity to witness
> for the Lord [to their extended families], as their
> people did not want it. However, Mr. Jubinville got
> all the children together and got them to sing sev-
> eral of the choruses which we had taught them, "*Jésus
> m'a tant aimé*" [the English equivalent chorus is "Be-
> cause he loved me so"], "*Oui, la victoire je l'aurai*"
> ["Yes, I shall have the victory"], "*Sous le sang,
> le précieux sang*" ["Under the blood, the precious
> blood"], and "*O, que ta main paternelle / Me bénisse
> à mon coucher*" ["May your Fatherly hand bless me as
> I sleep"]—a little bedtime prayer-chorus. . . . They
> told me it was really interesting to see the expres-
> sions on the faces. . . . I feel, as they do, that
> what the older ones could not do, these little ones
> have begun to do, to break down opposition. . . .
>
> Our Sunday evening services have not been very
> good [they were then beginning to meet in a rented
> building of a local Presbyterian Italian-language
> church], but we are having some good times in our
> individual contacts. Please continue to pray, as I
> know you do, for me. . . . It is my hope that the
> next four months will show vastly more progress than
> at present. I am really encouraged. . . . We have a
> little prayer meeting every Sunday before the ser-
> vice. As both Mr. St-Onge and Mr. Jubinville led in
> prayer [this past Sunday], I could not help but feel
> the nearness of the Lord. I hope to tackle the matter
> of a broadcast over the air. . . . I know . . . that
> it is ridiculous even to conceive the possibility of
> my getting such. But I rejoice in the word, "He hath
> chosen the weak things of the world to confound the
> mighty," and when we have it, men may wonder how, but

you and I shall know: that it may serve to remind us
"that no flesh should glory in his presence" but, "He
that glorieth, let him glory in the Lord."
    I close, with warmest affection in the bonds of
the gospel,

                              Yours most sincerely,
                              Thomas D. M. Carson

The correspondence between Tom and H. C. Slade of the
Union of Regular Baptists was full of hope. Money to support the
work came either through the Union office (in Toronto) or through
Snowdon Baptist Church in Montréal. All the costs of the literature
were borne by the Union, and records of exact accounting abound.
The records of Tom's management of various funds over the years
are not only scrupulous but remarkably detailed. A lovely note,
written to the Union office in February 1944, mentions three adults
by name and adds, "Undoubtedly one of the greatest experiences of
my life was to baptize these three French-Canadians Sunday morning. . . . The testimony of all was clear and strong."

No one foresaw the crisis that was just around the corner.

CHAPTER FOUR

CRISIS

*W*hen I began seminary study in Toronto in 1967, it was at a school called Central Baptist Seminary in Toronto, not Toronto Baptist Seminary where my parents had attended more than thirty years earlier. I knew that Central had grown out of TBS, or split off from it, toward the end of 1948. There had been some dispute or other about which I knew little and cared less. The first I heard about the details was in a course on Canadian Baptist history. Only then did I discover the role my father had played. When I next went home and confronted Dad with this account, I learned the most striking lesson of all: why he had never told me.

The story begins with two sets of unrelated events, events that came together to generate the most acute crisis Tom faced for many years.

By 1944 Tom was wondering if it would be wise for him to focus on one area of Montréal. The contacts he was following up were scattered all over the city; perhaps he should narrow his vision to one district, perhaps the St. Henri district. Correspondence went back and forth between Tom and the Union office in Toronto. In the Spring of 1945 a meeting was arranged in Montréal that brought together some of the senior figures in the Union with Tom to brainstorm (though they did not use that word) about the way ahead. All sides were seeing that a building would be necessary as well.

Before a decision was reached, however, Tom's help was

requested in another venture. In Drummondville, a city of about thirty thousand people (Greater Drummondville had about fifty thousand) only seventy miles east and slightly north of Montréal, a small group of English-speaking Christians were asking for pastoral help. Drummondville was at least 95 percent French and (of course) Catholic. The small English-language community had two or three churches, but none was even remotely evangelical. This small group of Christians met together in their homes and contacted the Union to see if someone could be sent to give them leadership, and perhaps at the same time plant something in French. The times of Tom's meetings in Montréal were adjusted, and from time to time he would spend Sunday evening leading a service in Drummondville.

By 1947 he was there just about every weekend. At the 1947 convention of the Union, he was formally asked to consider moving to Drummondville and starting a work there. Initially he stalled, uncertain what to do, but gradually his heart began to lean toward Drummondville. His correspondence shows that part of the appeal was the confined nature of the patch: fifty thousand in greater Drummondville versus two million in Montréal. The small English nucleus would give him a base while he started a French work, aiming for a bilingual church. For him the issue at the time was not the size of the field, but whether it had the potential to become a stable center from which other work might spring. "Our four years of experience trying to cover the huge area of greater Montréal has convinced us of the necessity of concentrating our efforts on a given centre in order to do French work most effectively" (letter dated 19 February 1948). Montréal could boast of a handful of other Christian workers. Drummondville had none, and it was one of several small cities in Les Cantons de l'Est ("The Eastern Townships") in need of French-speaking churches.

Perhaps most decisive to his thinking was the sudden availability of a building. This was a frame house on a substantial piece of property, a house large enough that two of its rooms could be adapted to make a small chapel while providing adequate space for his family to live in. This could be the beginning of a stable center.

In Montréal every effort to obtain an essential
building has thus far come to nought. But in Drummondville—greater Drummondville has a population of
some 50,000, 95 percent of whom are French-Canadian
Roman Catholics—we have a nucleus of Christians, to
whom it has been our privilege to minister from week
to week since last October, sufficiently interested
to look after the subsequent mortgage payments . . .
and who are anxious to see the work go ahead. Montréal will not be left uncultivated. But where we may
concentrate, there we believe we ought specially to
labour. (letter dated 19 February 1948)

The local group of believers in Drummondville provided the
initial five hundred dollars necessary to secure an option on the
building, with a further 4,500 dollars to be paid by 1 April 1948
or the option would expire. The Union approved the plan, not least
its Finance Committee. The Secretary-Treasurer of the Union, Rev.
Morley R. Hall, a man of great integrity with an enduring interest
in Québec, wrote a moving letter of appeal to the churches, dated
19 February 1948. Many churches pledged to send money to the
Union offices to buy the building in Drummondville, which would
be owned by the English-language church in Montréal, Snowdon
Baptist Church, until the Drummondville believers could be organized into a church. Tom signed the papers: backed by the Union,
the Drummondville believers were committed to buying the building.

The impending move to Drummondville and the purchase of
this building by the support of Union churches constituted one set
of events that set up the crisis about to break over Tom's head. The
other was a simmering problem precipitated by the increasingly
autocratic style of T. T. Shields.

It will be remembered that in the eyes of confessional Baptists,
Shields was the great hero of the 1920s controversy over McMaster
University. That conflict stamped him so powerfully that he focused
more and more of his energy on combating all perceived apostasy as
well as anything to do with Roman Catholicism. As early as 1932,
D. Martyn Lloyd-Jones had confronted him with the negativism
that was increasingly characterizing his ministry, exhorting him to

"preach the gospel to people positively and win them!"[1] Shields, moved by the directness of the challenge, promised to take the matter to his deacons and seek their counsel. They told him to keep on as he was doing, and that, regrettably, was what he did.

Worse was to come. Shields was by far the ablest preacher in the Union, and Jarvis Street Baptist Church by far the most influential church. Shields continued as the unchallenged president of the Union, even though his increasingly dictatorial approaches to all matters were beginning to alienate some pastors and churches. A few quietly withdrew. Those who confronted Shields in some open way inevitably lost the dispute.

In late 1947 or early 1948 Shields ordered—that is the right word—W. Gordon Brown, the man who officiated at the wedding of Tom and Margaret Carson nine years earlier and certainly the ablest teacher of Toronto Baptist Seminary, to join the pastoral team at Jarvis Street. Brown, then pastor of Runnymede Baptist Church while serving as dean at TBS, refused. If this had been the only autocratic step taken by Shields, doubtless it would have blown over. In fact, it was the last straw. Within the year W. Gordon Brown would start a rival seminary, Central Baptist Seminary. Close to 90 percent of the faculty and students joined him in the new venture. Shields was outraged at what he saw to be personal betrayal.

These two sets of events—Tom's impending move from Montréal to Drummondville and the developing drama in Toronto—came together in early 1948. Tom was never very political—indeed, in some ways he was naive—but when someone asked him, he gave his opinion that W. Gordon Brown was right not to acquiesce to Shields's demand. That information found its way back to T. T. Shields. Suddenly the Finance Committee of the Union set up a new Committee to pay for another trip to Drummondville and in due course announced its new conclusion that it had decided *not* to fund the Drummondville project. The Board of the Union sent out a printed letter to all the supporting churches justifying their decision and asking for their permission to put the money already

[1]Reported by Iain Murray, *D. Martyn Lloyd-Jones: The First Forty Years 1899–1939* (Edinburgh: Banner of Truth Trust, 1982), 271–274.

contributed into a fund for future development of the French work in Québec. They charged that Tom had gone ahead of formal approval, that the building was inappropriate, and much more of the same. Tom repeatedly contacted the Finance Committee and the Board, but without results. On 26 March 1948, just days before the deadline of 1 April when the next major installment was due, Tom was still trying to keep the matter private. He wrote a letter, which said in part:

I am making one more appeal, and am sending this letter to each member of the Finance Committee.

It seems almost incredible to me that the earnest effort of our churches in raising more than three thousand dollars in the space of five weeks expressly for the purpose of buying the property in Drummondville on which we have an option should be rendered useless by the refusal to release money for the purpose for which it was raised, and when it is most needed.

I have sought in vain for any justification of such an action in the record of the minutes and final resolution passed February 7, 1948 by the Finance Committee. . . . To some, certainly to the Secretary [Morley R. Hall], if one may judge by his appeal to the churches, the "earnest efforts" hinged on the procuring of the building so carefully selected, on which our Drummondville Christians had an option. . . .

Furthermore, the only building mentioned in the latest resolution was that building. It was requested "that an effort be made to obtain an extension of the option on the building previously considered until May 31st," implying, if it did not state, that that building was considered of real importance. . . .

Not many buildings are available to an aggressive Baptist work in the heart of Roman Catholic territory. . . . [The local curé vowed that there would never be a Protestant work in his parish. To preserve integrity, Tom had explained in detail to the Catholic seller what the building would be used for, as he did not want anyone to feel deceived.] Morley R. Hall wrote and spoke, and so also did I. There was no collusion between us. There was rather, of this I am sure, a true appreciation of the difficulties we face,

and a right understanding of the steps which must be
taken to do most effectually the Lord's work there.

The response has been most gratifying, more than
sufficient to close the deal tomorrow should the
churches' money sent in for this very purpose be released by the Finance Committee. . . .

Frankly, to withhold the monies sent in seems to
me nothing short of foolhardiness, and can only result in fearful repercussions among our churches who
have responded so generously to our appeal. I believe
from the depth of my heart and mind that the reason
for the so signal success of the campaign is that the
blessing of the Lord is upon it; that our churches
rejoice in the evident forward step taken in French-
Canadian evangelization; and that there is some measure of confidence, to say the least, in those of us
who have as strenuously as possible pressed the campaign. We earnestly pray that the Finance Committee
may take speedy action to send on the money.

Sincerely yours,
T. D. M. Carson

All to no avail. Tom scrambled to get the deadline extended by
a month. The vendor agreed on condition that another thousand
dollars be paid immediately. Tom borrowed the money as a personal loan (equivalent to more than half his annual salary). Then
on 20 April 1948 he sent the following letter to all the churches of
the Union:

Dear Brethren,

On behalf of the Drummondville Christians and myself
I want first of all to thank all the pastors, churches
and friends who so generously and heartily as unto
the Lord lent us their help, contributing more than
the $4,500 required to purchase the advantageous Drum-
mondville property under option. Besides the $4,383.48
actually received in the Union Office, some $400 was
given. The Lord did exceedingly above all that we
asked or thought, and we praise Him for it.

Nevertheless, after two meetings held April 6 and
16, by a majority vote on the 16th, the Board decided
not to proceed with purchase of the property, to
withhold the money, and to ask the churches that it

be turned aside to another use than that for which it was raised, accompanying their request with a letter of explanation.

This is the third or fourth time during the last few months that the Board's or Finance Committee's action or lack of it has left me with nearly no time whatsoever to act. As I had claimed in my letter to most of our churches that I had the backing of the Finance Committee I owe it to all concerned to give them an explanation. There is much more to it than the one-sided and extraordinary letter being sent out by the Board.

Their action, I have no doubt, is utterly bewildering to all our churches. In all fairness I ask that before they do anything with their gift other than that for which it was specifically raised . . . they at least will give me time, and await my statement.

At the moment, I have no time. In view of the Board's action I had no other recourse than to resign as a missionary under it, and carry on as the Lord enables the work which He gave me to do, to try to raise the $4,500 needed by April 21, that this challenging and unequalled opportunity might not be lost.

"There is no restraint to the LORD to save by many or by few." Several churches and individuals have rallied to our support so that, by advancing us money on the amounts now held up in the Union office, and by loans to us, we shall be able, "if the LORD delight in us," to proceed with purchase immediately.

As we expect to be moving to Drummondville in a week or two, please forward all contributions to

Rev. T. Carson
c/o Mr. Clarence Crook
Box 197
St-Simon de Drummond, Que.

Receipt from the Drummondville work will gladly be sent.

Thanking you once again, and praying God's richest blessing upon you, I remain,

Yours for French Canada,
T. D. M. Carson

So Tom was without his 1,800-dollar per annum salary, he had incurred serious debt, there was no certainty that the needed money would come through, and he and his family were moving from Verdun to Drummondville in a week's time.

Three days later, John R. Armstrong, pastor of Snowdon Baptist Church in Montréal, sent his own strong letter to all the churches, supporting Tom's request. About the same time, T. T. Shields wrote a lengthy letter to all the churches of the Union, giving his "take" on the situation and rebutting this brief letter from Tom. This was followed by a response to John Armstrong's letter, once again written by T. T. Shields. It included the paragraphs,

```
If Mr. Carson and Mr. Armstrong had deliberately
conspired together to disturb the peace of the
Union, and engender confusion in the minds of our
churches, it is difficult to see how they might
more effectively have done it than by the actions
they have taken.
    So far as I am concerned, with my many responsi-
bilities I would gladly have been relieved of all
executive responsibility in the Union right from the
beginning. I have accepted it only as a duty to co-
operate with my brethren in furthering the work of
the Union. But if it were attempted to carry on the
work of the Union by such irregular methods as have
been employed in this Drummondville matter, sooner or
later the Union's ship would be bound to pile up on
the rocks, a complete wreck.
```

On 5 May, Tom finally sent out his lengthy letter of explanation, running to eight pages of single-space typescript, run off on an old mimeograph machine. I have not included it here because of its length, but it is reproduced as an Appendix to this volume. By the time this letter was written, the Drummondville property had been purchased. Almost all of the churches that had pledged money sent it directly, sometimes demanding that what they had sent to the Union be returned to them, sometimes finding new money. Other churches and individuals chipped in. The letter happily and gratefully thanks those who have kept their pledges and then reports in detail all the steps that had brought them to this point. There is no mention of T. T. Shields by name—Tom refers to the lengthy circular letter from Shields as "the Board's letter"—and not a word of bitterness or reproach.

The churches were not exactly voting with their feet, as the expression goes, but with their checkbooks. The Secretary-Treasurer of the Union, Morley R. Hall, resigned: from his perspective, the Board had gone back on its pledge, and its action was "dishonourable" and "dishonest." T. T. Shields wrote a further letter to the churches, responding more briefly to Tom's lengthy explanation. In it he mentions the names of the mover and seconder of the crucial motion to rescind support—names carefully deleted from Tom's letter. They were "Rev. W. G. Brown" (still on the Executive Board and still the dean of Toronto Baptist Seminary) and "Rev. Stanley Wellington" (brother of Wilf Wellington, who entered work in French Canada about the same time as Tom). As for Morley R. Hall, Shields comments, "[I]t must be said that our worthy Secretary, Rev. Morley R. Hall, highly esteemed among us, aided and abetted Mr. Carson and Mr. Armstrong in all their irregular procedure."

In hindsight, one of the striking features of this dispute is that when the crucial vote by the Board was taken, two men with whom Tom was especially close, Morley R. Hall and W. Gordon Brown, were on opposite sides. Brown moved the motion; Hall resigned over it. But Tom's assessment of the situation turned on what he saw to be matters of principle. Any thought of challenging Shields personally was the farthest thing from his mind; conversely, despite his closeness to W. Gordon Brown (who had officiated at his wedding), Tom registered no sense of personal betrayal. It was simply a matter of principle.

In the aftermath, a lengthy correspondence opened up between Tom and Morley R. Hall, who, while taking on pastoral responsibilities in Hamilton, worked tirelessly to find support for the fledgling work in Drummondville. It also generated lengthy correspondence between Tom and W. Gordon Brown, including some moving exchanges strangely blessed with both candor and the reserved courtesy of the day. Brown decided Tom had been right. The church of which he was still pastor (while he was also serving as dean of Toronto Baptist Seminary), Runnymede Baptist, started sending additional support money to Tom, as the latter was no longer being supported by the Union. Many of their letters simply talk about the progress of the gospel in their own patches. But the clash over Drummondville became the trigger that precipitated a raft of decisions. W. Gordon Brown withdrew from Toronto Baptist Seminary and by the end of 1948 started Central Baptist Seminary (initially called Canadian Baptist Seminary). Shields was so angry that he shut the doors of TBS to students and faculty who bolted, so they could not collect even their personal belongings. Tom's counsel was to accept the loss, speak softly, weep over the deterioration of a great leader, and move on. The fledgling church in Drummondville put the new seminary into its mission budget.

Perhaps more importantly, a document dated 14 February 1949 reads as follows:

> While recognizing our deep debt of gratitude to Dr. T. T. Shields in his past exploits in the defence of the Gospel, the undersigned brethren, all pastors of Union Churches, deeply regret that they find it necessary to express their profound disagreement with him in his recent dismissal and official denunciation of Dean Brown and discover that their confidence in him as a leader and as President of the Union of Regular Baptist Churches of Ontario and Québec has been destroyed.

The statement is extraordinarily strong, for the fifty names that follow (more were added later) are not those of rabble-rousers and hotheads, but some of the most sober-minded and thoughtful leaders of the day. Had action been taken to require Shields to step down, doubtless the Union as it then was would still have been preserved. In fact, however, he hung on until his death in 1955. The Union substantially disintegrated, and from the pieces was formed, in 1953, the Fellowship of Evangelical Baptist Churches in Canada. The first General Secretary was Morley R. Hall. A handful of good men remained with the Union, of course, but the Union itself became a shadow of its former self.

Tom foresaw none of this. He was not a great strategist; he was simply a pastor committed to the gospel, to evangelism, and to principled integrity. Yet in the eyes of many of the Baptist leaders of that generation, the Drummondville affair is precisely what precipitated the unraveling of the Union and the formation of the Fellowship, and it contributed to the founding of Central Baptist Seminary.

The main outline of these developments I learned when, about twenty years later, I was a student at Central Baptist Seminary. Reflecting on the abuse that Tom had absorbed without retaliation, the lecturer ended his survey of these developments with the comment, "One of the first things I want to see when I get to heaven is Tom Carson's crown."

I had not heard a whisper of these events at home. It had occasionally struck me as a bit odd that Dad, who was an ordinary pastor, seemed to be on a first-name basis with most of the perceived leaders of the Fellowship, considering that most of them were pastors of much larger ministries and had often held high office in the national association. But I had not thought deeply about my observation. From my parents I had only heard positive things about T. T. Shields. I can still remember Mum summarizing some of his sermons from the 1930s when she had been a student at TBS. I recall her reflections on his sermon "Other Little Ships," which became the title of one of his books of sermons. The McMaster controversy of the 1920s was faithfully recounted to me, but nothing of the Drummondville affair. My siblings were similarly ignorant.

So the next time I went home, I brought this matter up. The conversation went something like this:

Me: "I've been learning some interesting Baptist history from 1948–1949."

Dad: "Oh?"

Me: "It seems you had a pretty significant part to play."

Dad: "What were you told?

So I summarized the events as I understood them, though of course at that point I had seen none of the primary documents.

Dad: "I suppose that's pretty close to what happened."

Me: "So how come you never told us kids any of this?"

Dad (after a long pause): "There were two reasons. First, you were children of the manse, and although you have seen the outworking of the gospel, you have also seen more than your share of difficult and ugly things, and we did not think it wise to expose you to this history when you were young. Second, Marg and I decided we needed to protect our own souls from bitterness. So we took a vow that neither of us would ever say an unkind thing about T. T. Shields. And we have kept our vow."

A recent note from my sister Joyce comments, "As I look back on life with Mom and Dad, perhaps the one thing I recall most vividly is the memory that I don't have. Try as I might, I cannot recollect one time when either of them spoke negatively about another person. Although Mom was an extremely astute judge of character, her analyses were well seasoned with grace and the latent potential for redemption."

CHAPTER FIVE

THE EARLY
DRUMMONDVILLE YEARS

*B*y the end of 1949, Tom and Marg had three children. At six, Joyce was the oldest; the youngest, Jim, was born in the summer of that year. I was squeezed between the two. With a young family and a fledgling bilingual church, Tom and Marg had their hands full.

They remained in Drummondville until the autumn of 1963—a total of fifteen years. During the last four years or so of that period, Tom was facing another kind of crisis: his own dark night of the soul. That dark night also marks the beginning of his journals. Before taking up that account in the next chapter, I shall here survey Tom's first ten or eleven years in Drummondville, both in terms of the church and of the experience of his family.

The Church

In a letter to W. Gordon Brown dated 16 May 1949, Tom writes in part:

> The attendances [last Sunday] were good. In the morn-
> ing we had thirty-eight out, the most for any Sunday
> since coming here. I just noticed [from my records]
> that there were fifteen in our first Sunday, just
> one year ago. In that way there is great reason for
> encouragement. While we did not emphasize the an-
> niversary in the French [evening] service, we were

grateful that there were eleven out, seven of whom
were French-Canadians. Three of these were a family
who I thought had definitely decided to return to the
R.C. church. Our S.S. had nineteen. There were five
one year ago.

In a letter dated 25 September 1949, a month after his youngest
son had been born, Tom wrote to John F. Dempster, the pastor of
his "home" church in Ottawa. I include some paragraphs from it
followed by a couple of reflections:

Dear John,

Since your return from your holidays at the end of
August I have been intending to write to you. We received a cheque for 100.25 in July, another in August, and a third has just come through this month
from Calvary [Baptist Church in Ottawa] towards our
support. Without this help, humanly speaking, I do
not see how we should have managed, and I repeat
again, what I have said so often, which does not go
deep enough—thank you. Please pass on our grateful
acknowledgement to the church.

On September 7 I baptized a Christian woman, one of
our English-speaking Christians from Drummondville,
in Emmanuel church [in Montréal]. The same week, or
the beginning of the next week, I was visiting with a
man whom I have frequently visited since coming here—
a Roman Catholic. During the course of our conversation he said to me, "Mr. Carson, Jesus is my Saviour;
I want to be baptized; and I want also to send in my
abjuration to the Roman Catholic Church." I had spoken to him about these matters at other times, but
had not mentioned them this visit. It came as a great
piece of news when it thus burst from him. He thinks
of himself as being English-speaking, although he
speaks English with a strong French accent. These
are two encouraging pieces of news which we have just
lately had. I was also thinking that our French work
is picking up; more are attending, and even showing
more interest. Tonight, however, there was a drop to
almost none in the attendance. This is French work.
However, the Spirit is moving. . . .

[Regarding the forthcoming annual Convention,
which had pastors churning over what was widely per-

The Early Drummondville Years

fice in Toronto:] There is no doubt that all this is
sending us back to a renewed, perhaps new, grasp of
the sovereignty and independence of the local church,
and being jealous for her independence and sovereignty. The "church . . . is the pillar and ground of the
truth." And any affiliation we shall have with any
group of New Testament churches, in very many cases,
will be after due consideration if such affiliation
is going to affect adversely the local church. Not
that it is our idea that we should join on condition
we get something out of it; but the progress and development of local churches—not their splitting and
destruction—is of paramount consideration.

I was in Ottawa a week ago Friday night. I was going to telephone, but I just seemed lackadaisical.
(Thought I'd look that up in the dictionary: it is
not quite what I mean: "Languishing, affected, given
to airs & graces, feebly sentimental"! Well, maybe
I was "languishing.") We had a good conference in
French at Noranda. There are some fine French-Canadian converts.

The letter contains many hints of Tom's condition and thoughts at the time. First, transparently Tom and Marg were hard up financially. I shall come back to this reality from which they did not escape for the next decade and a half. Second, the building in Drummondville was, after all, designed to be a home; so it is not surprising that there was no baptistery. Indeed, it took some time before the believers there had the assets to convert two parlors into one chapel that could comfortably seat about sixty people. The rest of the house was in effect the parsonage—though on Sundays, Bible classes found themselves in our kitchen, another common room, sometimes my parents' bedroom, and downstairs in the basement. It took several more years before there were adequate assets to build a baptistery under the platform at the front of the chapel. Tom did all the carpentry construction, including building the immensely strong support needed for the baptistery when it was filled with water. Third, Tom was maintaining close links with churches in Montréal. Doubtless this was partly stirred by the lack of a baptistery. Nevertheless the closest Union church with a baptistery was in Montréal, seventy miles away. Emmanuel Baptist Church, to which the congregation resorted for the baptism described in the letter, was in Verdun, part of greater Montréal, and was, of course, Tom's first charge out of seminary. The alternative was Snowdon Baptist Church, which also opened its facilities from time to time.

Fourth, this was still a day of small but steady progress. Transparently this buoyed Tom's spirits. He did not know that the hardest days were still ahead of him. Fifth, his reflections on the ongoing struggles that the churches were having with the Union are cast not in terms of winning and losing, still less in terms of personalities and conflicts, but in terms of New Testament ecclesiology as he understood it within his own Baptist heritage. Even so, his insistence on the autonomy of the local church was never unqualified. The Drummondville congregation was established under the Union (even though the head office of the Union was a bit wobbly in its support) and would soon be a part of the Fellowship. Its name would be Faith Baptist Church (Église Baptiste de la Foi). Sixth, his musings on the meaning of the word *lackadaisical* reflect his lifelong interest in words and their meanings, both in English and French. Tom was always more interested in words than in, say, discourse or literary genre. This in turn reflected a mind rather more devoted to the tiny detail than to the big picture. Seventh, the letter discloses that Tom was still traveling quite a bit—in this case Montréal, Ottawa, and Noranda. These were all undertaken in line with his calling, of course: to undertake baptisms, to visit supporting churches, and to attend a conference relevant to the French work. And eighth, the reference to the conference in Noranda and to French-Canadian converts there reminds us that other workers were taking up the challenge of French Canada.

This last point deserves some exploration. When Tom began his full-time ministry in French Canada, there were only three such pastors connected with the Union, and no more than a handful in the entire Province. Now a steady trickle of new men was being added to their number. Most of these were Canadians or Americans who had to learn the language and culture of Québec, but within a few more years these included two or three who were themselves French Canadians (e.g., Gabriel Cotnoir, Yvon Hurtubise, Ernest Houle, and, a little later, Fernand Petit-Clerc). Some studied for a time at Institut Biblique Béthel (Bethel Bible Institute), a tiny school near Sherbrooke in the Emmaus Bible School tradition (Plymouth Brethren) that offered courses both in French and in introductory Bible and theology.

This was an extraordinary group of strong-minded individuals with very different styles, working in highly diverse communities. William Frey from Switzerland eventually settled in Montréal. By 1958 he was joined by Elisée Beau from France, who after two years in Toronto at Central Baptist Seminary moved to francophone Canada and planted a church on the south shore of Montréal. He became a crucial figure in developing camp ministries. In the north, the Heron brothers were busy evangelizing and getting thrown into jail; in the south, Wilson Ewin and Ernie Keefe were facing similar experiences. In the early 1950s, Baptist ministers spent a total of about eight years in jail. Nevertheless, small churches were being started and were gradually taking root.

It was a day of mighty efforts, some of them courageous, with mostly small results. Two or three of these relatively new pastors wrote spectacularly interesting prayer letters to their anglophone constituents and sending agencies, making a great deal out of every tiny gospel advance but almost never reporting the failures and disappointments, the spurious conversions and instances of falling away owing to lack of perseverance. Some years later, when supporters from English Canada visited these congregations, they were often surprised and bewildered, not to say let down, when they saw the paucity of enduring results. For better or for worse, that was not Tom's style: he was scrupulously faithful and evenhanded in his reports. Another relative newcomer embarked on a scheme that mobilized the entire team. He found the names and addresses of all French-Canadian Catholic priests, monks, nuns, and teaching brothers, about sixteen thousand of them, and wrote each of them a series of three letters, each about five pages long. A copy of one of them is in front of me as I type these lines, a letter dated 20 October 1958. To avoid possible detection and interception, the letters were addressed by hand and mailed from many different locations. All of us Carson kids can remember participating with other folk in Drummondville, assembly-line fashion, folding, stuffing, sealing, and sorting hundreds of these letters. There was no massive realignment because of these bold moves, but there were many individual exchanges with various Catholic clergy, most of them cordial and respectful on both sides. A few left the Catholic Church, and usually left Québec as well: the pressures on them were too great if they remained.[1]

A few of the men who entered the work during that period eventually burned out. One or two rugged individualists swerved toward isolation, their "lone ranger" attitudes picking up forms of extremism. But most of them were there for the long haul, and many exercised wise leadership for decades. As they started up, most of them would spend time with Tom, for by now he was widely perceived to be one of the veterans. It was during this period that I first met Bill Phillips, with whom, a decade and a half later, I would have my third internship, helping him plant the church in Ahuntsic (a district of Montréal) in 1969. Bill had suffered from polio as a child and fought the increasing disability with extraordinary courage and grace, enormously sustained by his wife Blanche.[2]

My first meeting with the man under whom I served my first internship, Ernie Keefe, had a rather different character. I was just a lad. Dad was out, and Mum, never very strong, often needed a rest in the afternoon. On this day she told me that a couple of pastors were going to arrive at the door, and would I let them into the living room and talk with them until she got up from the rest she needed. These two men, one of them Ernie Keefe, arrived as announced, and I let them in. We had barely sat down when one of them asked me, "Do you know where we were last night?" I didn't have a clue and said so. They smiled and said, "In jail."

---

[1] For a handful of interesting accounts of this sort, see chapter 13 of Élisée Beau, *Une vie sous l'appel du Berger: Autobiographie d'Élisée Beau*, second edition (Montréal: Éditions SEMBEQ, 2007), 84–89.

[2] His little book *Modern Day Missionary Miracles: A History of the Ministry of the Fellowship of Evangelical Baptist Churches in Canada in the Province of Québec* (Montréal: Fellowship French Mission, 1998) is still the best survey of these years. No detailed historical study has been written.

Our house regularly attracted more than its share of troubled people, partly because the chapel and the home were one building, and partly because Dad was a soft touch. When he returned a couple of hours later, Mum informed him that a couple of "jailbirds" were in the living room. Dad almost panicked until he discovered who they were. That night was bitterly cold. True to his nature, Tom insisted that the visitors put their car in the garage, leaving his outside in the cold. In the middle of the night, the gas station next door to us went up in flames. There was serious danger that the fire would spread to our garage and then to our house. Inside, we kids were bundled up in our warmest winter clothes in case we had to flee. We gazed out the windows at the flames and explosions leaping in the cold a few yards away—and between the window and the flames, Tom and our visitors were trying to change a tire on Tom's car in the -20° Fahrenheit weather, so they could move it and get the other car out of the garage to safety. In this way various friendships and partnerships in the gospel were forged. Ernie Keefe himself planted a church in Asbestos-Danville, about thirty miles away.

All of this gospel activity, though it was an enormous improvement on the situation a decade and a half earlier, had the strange effect of in some way marginalizing Tom. Part of his thinking in pushing ahead with the Drummondville work, it will be recalled, was to provide a center out of which other work could grow. It seemed so eminently reasonable. But other work was growing up, admittedly slowly, in such a way as to start new centers. Drummondville was not more strategic than other places. In one sense it was less so: it was a bilingual work, which meant that Tom's energies were somewhat dissipated. The advantage of the bilingual approach when Tom moved to Drummondville was that the English folk constituted a small group with which to begin, providing the backing to purchase a building and get going. Indeed, a number of other works around Québec sprang up using the same strategy. But most of the new French works developing around the Province were exclusively French. Tom's strategy may have been helpful for a short period of time, but it was now increasingly eclipsed. It was perceived to be hindering the development of francophone leaders. Within another decade or so the bilingual churches would all become exclusively francophone. In the 1950s, however, these things were still working themselves out.

Moreover, some of the other workers gained a certain cachet either because of their superlative prayer letters or because they had endured prison time. It was not Tom's nature to indulge in the former, and he was spared the latter. Occasionally he was hassled by the police in Drummondville, but that was rare. Once or twice one of his children was beaten up as "*maudits* Protestants" ("damned Protestants"), but that too was rare. He diligently tried to start a radio program on a local French-language station. All but two of the governing board of the station approved; the two who disapproved were priests, and Tom never got on. Never in our hearing, and certainly not in his papers, did Tom express any jealousy of or malice toward other ministers who seemed to be eclipsing him, but whether he realized it or not the way was being paved to generate in him a feeling of inferiority with which he would wrestle for the rest of his life. Compared with some of the more dramatic turns around him, his ministry was ordinary.

Another factor played a part. During the 1950s and 1960s the Baptists and the Plymouth Brethren were the only significant workers in Québec, and they grew at about the same slow rate. A little later on, Pentecostals, Mennonite Brethren, a handful of Presbyterians, Free Church workers, and others were added to the pot. The relationships between the Baptists and the Brethren varied enormously from place to place around the Province. In Drummondville, the Brethren began their work some time after Tom had arrived, and for quite a number of years they systematically visited all of the French-speaking members of the fledgling Baptist church in an effort to win them over. The appeal was not only theological (they held that they operated with an ecclesiology more in line with the New Testament documents) but cultural and nationalistic: theirs was an *exclusively* French-speaking work. The problem was only exacerbated when one of the few Baptist pastors who was a French-speaking Québecker "defected" to the Brethren side and gave guidance to the Brethren cause in Drummondville.

Tom tried to guard his own flock, but he scrupulously avoided any temptation to play the sheep-stealing game himself. These developments nevertheless generated their own stresses. These were added to the broader challenges faced by most of the nascent French-speaking churches. It was not uncommon for converts to be ostracized by their families, and if they ran their own small business, they could easily be shut down. In Drummondville, fairly early in the 1950s a shoemaker with his own thriving shop in St-Cyrille, a village that was part of greater Drummondville, was wonderfully converted, along with his wife. As soon as his conversion became clear to his neighbors, the local priest applied pressure, and he lost 90 percent of his business. He struggled to carry on. Some months later, in the middle of the night, his shop was burned to the ground. The authorities acknowledged it had been torched, but of course no one was ever arrested and charged. The couple decided to leave the area and resettled in English-speaking Windsor, Ontario, seven hundred miles away. They remained in friendly and grateful contact with Tom for the rest of their lives, but of course their departure did nothing to help establish the French congregation in Drummondville. In the 1950s such stories were not uncommon in Québec. Even where the opposition was less dramatic, believers were often sneeringly labeled as *les hérétiques, les communistes*, or the like.

The Family

The dynamics and stresses of these developments slid past the Carson children without our understanding, of course. The events themselves could not be hidden from us: the drama of the shoe-maker's departure, for example. Yet our parents unpacked in front of the children few of the pressures they were facing.

When we first arrived in Drummondville, Joyce was only five years old. She could speak no French, and one of the neighbor-hood boys, a year or two older, doubly provoked because she was a "damned Protestant" and because she couldn't speak his language, resolved the issue by beating her up every time she went outside to play. Dad solemnly insisted that she turn the other cheek. Less convinced that this was the sort of situation Jesus had in mind, and with a surer grasp of playground dynamics than Dad enjoyed, Mum quietly told her only daughter that should this happen again, she was to roll her hand into a fist and hit her tormenter once, as hard as she could, and then come in and tell Mum. This she did. The problem was instantly solved. The two children learned to play together, and the boy grew up to be a star in the National Hockey League.

Meals were for conversation as well as for food, and while topics were suitably diverse, they often became theological. Dad liked to explain things. Usually family devotions took place after the evening meal. Everyone had to have a Bible because each person read a verse, turn and turn about, invariably starting with Mum, until the chapter or other unit was finished. Older friends remember little Jimmy, still in a high chair, holding his Bible, required to "read" his verse when his turn came around by repeating the words, phrase by phrase, as another member of the family read them out to him. This part of the exercise was inviolable, regardless of visitors, including friends from school, all of whom had to be given a Bible and participate by reading his or her verse as it came up. Most often Dad led in prayer; sometimes it was Mum; rarely it was everyone in the family.

Following family devotions, if Dad was not too busy we could prevail on him, when we were very young, to stand on his head, using an old green pillow, and then help us to do the same. This could end in squeals of laughter and assorted silliness. Less often time was set aside for games. Dad loved these times. He was pretty competitive, but we soon learned two things: play by the rules (and if these were in dispute, we had to look them up), and be a good sport. No one would cheer more enthusiastically if someone else won than Dad. Sunday afternoons, even if Dad was preaching that night (as he almost invariably was), found him reserving time, often while Mum was having a rest, for a wide variety of knowledge games: Bible trivia, historical trivia ("When was the Battle of Hastings?"), and so on. Years later when his first grandchildren came along (Joyce's girls), Grandpa could be found carefully teaching them how to play Monopoly or some other game.

For all her wisdom, Mum was spectacularly uncoordinated and never played sports with us. Dad taught us to skate, swim, catch a ball, play table tennis, and the like. Joyce writes, "I can remember him . . . trying to get me to keep my focus on winning footraces when my main concern was perusing the audience to make certain everyone was watching." Even when he was an old man, if a lake were nearby and the temperature appropriate, Dad would be unlikely to miss his early morning swim of half a mile or so. When the older two children had left home, Jim, still in high school, took up wrestling and proceeded to demonstrate his developing skills by practicing on his fifty-year-old father. He ended up breaking his Dad's little finger, leaving it crooked for the remainder of his days. Dad would use that finger to point out things in documents, inviting people to ask the inevitable question, "What happened to your finger?" He would take pride in explaining that his son did that to him while wrestling. (As for me, I have learned to quit while I'm ahead. It was time to quit when my own son, already a U.S. Marine, gently asked, "Do you have any idea, Dad, how many ways I could kill you with my bare hands?")

Music was important. We sang around the piano, usually in English, sometimes in French. Usually Dad played, until Joyce outstripped him. I doubt that there was a single song in Sankey's hymnbook that we did not know—all twelve hundred of them. Mum had an excellent soprano voice; all of us learned to sing parts and play instruments, though Joyce was the only one who was gifted.

Discipline was coordinated between Mum and Dad: it was almost impossible to play one against the other. Inevitably they sometimes got things wrong, but not often. We were never allowed, under any circumstances, to sass Mum. Disobedience and disrespect were lumped together and were punishable. Occasionally we were disciplined for attitude. Whining and other ways of making life miserable for others were not tolerated.

Throughout all his years, Tom never had a study outside the home. Usually a single room was reserved for the purpose, though for one extended period of time this was sacrificed to the needs of his elderly mother-in-law. When the door to the study was shut, we kids knew we were not to intrude. Dad's practice in private prayer was to kneel before the big chair that he used and pray loudly enough to vocalize, so as to keep his mind from wandering. Outside the door we could hear him praying, even if we could not hear what he was saying. I can remember countless days when he prayed for forty-five minutes or more; strange to tell, at this juncture I cannot recall days when he didn't. Jim recalls barging into Dad's study unannounced, finding him on his knees praying, and quietly backing out. "But that image has always remained with me, especially during my later, rebellious teen years. While walking away from God, I could not get away from the image of my father on his knees, praying for me. It is one of the things that eventually brought me back."

For all of his efforts to play with his children, in some ways Dad was a very private individual. He did not encourage intimate conversation. Partly, I suspect, he was simply reflecting his own times. Understood that way, it was amazing how much time he gave us. But there were exceptional times of bonding. Joyce remembers the long letter he wrote when she turned twenty-one. Jim remembers a time when Mum was hospitalized for about two weeks and was incapacitated for a third. The older two kids were farmed out with friends or relatives. (I stayed with older cousins in Montréal. There I learned to play chess and came back and infected the family and several friends with the chess virus.) Jim was kept at home, "a special time of bonding, never again experienced."

By today's standards we were shockingly poor. Mum had an older sister who was married to a policeman, a big man who stood about 6'4". More than once one of his suits, somewhat used, would be passed on to Mum, who would remove all thread and hems, lay out on the disassembled fabric the pattern for Dad, who stood 5'7½", and cut it out and make up a suit on her treadle Singer sewing machine. Also, in those early years a fair bit of time would be devoted to making up preserves from summer fruits and vegetables. Despite extended illnesses in the family, which sometimes cost huge amounts of money that we did not have, Dad and Mum would pray, and somehow the money would come in, to the last cent. Dad and Mum made no big deal of this; they were simply quietly grateful. I think they were afraid to enlarge upon the fiscal pressures, partly because they did not want their children to grow up complaining that they were poor, and partly because they wanted their children to grow up simply *expecting* God to provide what was necessary. Self-pity and greed were to be eschewed at all costs. I was probably particularly slow in this regard—it was not until I became a student at McGill University that it dawned on me one day, as I saw what I was wearing and what others had, that I came from a poor family. Yet the Lord provided special treats. Virtually every summer we had a week's vacation, either at Muskoka Baptist Conference in Ontario (where pastors of small works supported by the Fellowship were given a free week) or at a family holiday cabin across the border in New Hampshire, where the owner gave us a free week in gratitude to Tom for his ministry some years earlier. My recollection of Dad in all this is that he was characterized by disciplined and unwavering gratitude.

Dad's mind was so full of Scripture—he spent quite a lot of time memorizing his Bible in both English and French—that not infrequently he addressed us in biblical quotations, even when they were, strictly speaking, out of context. The text itself had become the stuff of his verbal apparatus, with the result that this was the language he naturally deployed when he had something to say. If one of us kids was pontificating on some subject of which we knew almost nothing (when did ignorance ever stop children and fools from pronouncing their opinions?), Dad would patiently hear us out, smile, and comment, "He wist not what to say" (Mark 9:6). Modern translations render this, "He did not know what to say," describing Peter's ignorant remark at the Transfiguration, blurted out when he should have kept silent. If any of us complained about the weather, Dad could be counted on to recite, "This is the day which the LORD hath made; we will rejoice and be glad in it" (Psalm 118:24). He knew, of course, that the "day" in the psalm's context is the time when the stone that the builders rejected becomes the "head stone." Nevertheless his affirmation of God's sovereignty even over the weather found happy expression in the quoted line, a sentence we heard on many occasions.

Dad was always quick to criticize any speech or behavior in his children that seemed to tarnish God's glory, question his wisdom, or make light of his Word; yet almost always he did so without ultimatums or threatening outbursts. One Saturday we were both weeding a flower bed. I was in first year of high school, I think, and going through my first poetry-writing phase. I wrote for my own amusement but sometimes printed the results in the school newspaper. Observing the worms as I was hoeing, I thought it would be fun to write a poem in the first person from a worm's point of view. I composed it in my head on the spot: a worm appreciating the warmth of the sun, squeezing through particles of dirt, etc. My last two lines were, "I saw the spade flash in the sun: / Woe is me! I am undone." I thought it was hilarious and could hardly wait to print it at school. I interrupted my weeding long enough to recite it proudly to my father. He kept on weeding, said nothing for a minute or two, and then quietly asked, "Are you quite sure you want to print a poem that applies to a worm the deepest reflections of the prophet Isaiah when he was afforded a vision of the transcendent God in all his glory?"

"It's just a joke," I protested. But I never printed the poem.

Reflections on how Dad and Mum related to each other can wait until the chapter on Mum's Alzheimer's disease.

For the moment, Jim's final reflections on Dad in the home are worth recording:

> When all is said and done, what image stands out most of all? It is of Father laughing. A big hearty smile, eyes crinkled up, face red, shoulders raised. He had the best laughter lines of anyone I've ever known. Whatever hurtful memories there may be, they are overshadowed by these thoughts. He could laugh at almost anything, especially including himself. And the second thought is of him talking or singing to himself as he would go about doing things, or messing around in the basement.

The reason this perspective is so important is that it must be integrated with the increasing gloom that was marking Dad's interior life, a gloom that he kept from everyone except Mum.

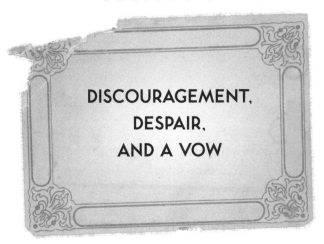

CHAPTER SIX

DISCOURAGEMENT, DESPAIR, AND A VOW

*B*y the summer of 1959, Joyce was only one year away from leaving home, and I was entering high school. In Africa, something took place that had its own quiet impact on the work in Québec.

In March 1959 the riots in Léopoldville warned missionaries and others in the Belgian Congo that the country was likely to be restive and perhaps dangerous for a while. These riots were part of the process that brought about the Congo's emancipation from its colonial power in June 1960. Many missionaries returned home for a while. Some of them were Americans, of course, and the most experienced of them brought with them knowledge of both a tribal language and of French. Under the influence of Belgium, French was the language of education in the Congo, especially advanced education. Some of these missionaries, looking around for another francophone part of the world where they might serve until they could return to the Congo, began to think of Québec.

A handful came north, and their arrival infused some of the long-standing missionaries and pastors with fresh hope. By and large the French churches were holding their own, but not much more. It was a time of slogging perseverance rather than advance or even the frisson of dangerous opposition. These former missionaries to French West Africa might not know the nuances of Canadian culture, but if they were fluent in French it surely would not take them too long to integrate and then put their shoulders to the plow.

Not one of them lasted more than six months. As a high school student, I saw myself as more than equipped to venture opinions on just about everything. So I asked Dad why none of them had the courage and stamina to stick it out.

Always the meekest of men, Dad replied rather mildly, "Don, you have to understand that they have been used to serving in a part of the world where they have seen much blessing. They are used to considerable crowds, they have built clinics and hospitals, they have seen many people converted and helped to train pastors to teach them. Then they arrive here and find everything to be interminably slow. How are they likely to read this, except to conclude that they must have misunderstood their call to Québec since no fruit seems to be forthcoming?"

"So," I replied, "why don't you go to some part of the world where there would be much fruit instead of staying here and producing so little?"

Until then the conversation had been casual. Now he wheeled on me and said rather curtly, "I stay because I believe God has many people in this place"—referring, of course, to the encouragement God gave to Paul in Corinth (Acts 18:10). This was one of many times when Tom grounded his perseverance in the doctrine of election.

In addition to the apparent stagnation of the work, other factors contributed to Tom's growing discouragement. The building housed both our home and the chapel, and Tom ended up doing repairs and maintenance for both. By temperament he tended to focus on little jobs immediately at hand rather than on strategic priorities, and this tendency certainly worsened as his discouragement grew. Breaking out of the cycle seemed mountainous. I am not sure if by today's standards he would be diagnosed as suffering from clinical depression, for on all public fronts he continued to function well enough that few people, other than his wife, discerned the turmoil. But intermingled with these sorts of things was a spiritual dimension: he prayed, but sometimes the heavens seemed as hard and closed as brass. He was no less committed to the French work than he had ever been. The four years from 1959, when his journals begin, to 1963, when the family left Drummondville and moved to Hull, are by far the bleakest parts of his writings. But although the zest for challenges had dissipated and the joy of the Lord peeped through only intermittently, not once is there a suggestion that he missed his calling or that he wished to abandon ministry in francophone Canada.

Part of Tom's initial purpose in keeping a journal was to strengthen the self-disciplined use of his time.

Monday, Nov. 9, 1959

[After detailing everything he had done so far that day]: Why do I write these details? Because it seems to me now important to keep a careful record of my daily "accomplishments" or otherwise, if ever I am to overcome in the work of God.

My present plan calls for four hours study on my preaching and teaching ministry in the mornings, at least two and a half hours visitation in the afternoons, plus the extra time either for more such study or for work relating to visitation. The evenings may be answering all correspondence, preparing "The Faith" [regular church paper, coined because the church was called Faith Baptist Church], reading books, articles, building around the property—in other words, anything, including study and visitation which could be helpful, relaxing. . . .

Prayer, the main source of strength of all, must find its necessary time in the early hours of the day, in the evening, around meal hours, without intruding on this ministry of teaching, preaching and visitation. Yet it must undergird all the ministry.

I propose to write carefully, regularly, and fully so that my life may be weighed in the balances of my own consciousness and conscience, and by God's grace I may eliminate the many pockets of weakness that are sapping my spiritual strength, undermining my ministry, and—let me say it—DESTROYING SOULS. God help me.

Monday, Nov. 16, 1959

Visited and saw Mrs. S. last Tuesday afternoon. She is being pursued by Jehovah's Witnesses, as are the B.s. Lord, help me.

Yesterday, Sunday, saw Mr. B. (Sr.), Mrs. V.B.
(Jr.), whose Diane is sick, called at B.s and M.B.s
in Windsor Mills. How few of these professing Christians are on the ball. The pastor sets the example.

This morning I rose at 7:30 A.M. Had prayer after
9:30 for three-quarters of an hour, but the heavens
seem brass. That was why finally Saul went to the
Witch of Endor. O God, have mercy upon me according to
Thy loving-kindness. . . . [Tom then describes more
than half a dozen whom he has been visiting and for
whom he has been praying. But in his mind he has not
been doing enough: two or three have died recently,
and he views their unconverted state at death as the
result of his own laxness.] I have no excuse. The
blood of so many is on my head! I'm afraid and defeated. "The fearful shall have their part in the lake
which burneth with fire and brimstone: which is the
second death." Yet I can do nothing to help myself.
Every effort to overcome through the years has failed;
every effort I make now will likewise fail. If God
does not put a new spirit within me I am as helpless
as if I were dead. I need relief. I need the way of escape from my temptation. What is it? And where is it?

Tuesday, Nov. 17, 1959

In working yesterday afternoon on clearing my basket,
my heart, so dreadfully expressed in the morning, was
lifted up a little. $25.00 was received from H. H.
marked personal use. How close we are running things,
yet God is being so generous to us. In the evening
I visited Mrs. I., still really sick in bed. . . .
Straightened [the church's financial] books with Mr.
Conyers. Sunday night I learned Mrs. G. is interested
in joining the church. Lord, help me to be faithful
here: we'd like to have her—truly converted—with us.

This morning I read Jer. 1 & 2. When God sent
Jeremiah, He said [and here Tom quotes the Synodale
French version: in addition to the English KJV and
the French Segond versions, Tom read the Bible right
through in version after version], "Say not, I am a
child: for thou shalt go to find all that I shall
send thee, and whatsoever I command thee thou shalt
speak." Again, God says, "See, I have this day given
you all power over the nations . . ." [I have cited
the KJV, adapting it to reflect the French Synodale].

> Out of weakness Jeremiah is made strong. Then the
> note on the almond tree [Jeremiah 1:11–12] is in-
> structive: "The almond tree . . . begins to flower
> and wake up from winter's sleep before the other
> trees, beginning in the month of January. Because
> of this, the blossoming almond is called in Hebrew
> [šāqēd] 'the tree that watches' [just as Yahweh 'is
> watching' [šōqēd] over his word]. This tree is thus
> the symbol of divine vigilance."
> The expression "Where is the LORD?" (Jer. 2:6,
> 8 and often in the OT) [the French version reg-
> ularly translates the Tetragrammaton with "Où est
> l'Éternel?", i.e. "Where is the Eternal One?"] is a
> symbol of trust, of going in search of the Lord, not
> of unbelief. Cf. 2 K. 2, Elisha.
> And what of sin? "For you know how to find your
> way, to seek love" [my translation of the Synodale,
> which rightly reflects the Hebrew]: how much [irony]
> is in this expression (Jer. 2:33). But note what fol-
> lows . . . : "Thus you have arrived at the place where
> you are comfortable with evil." Let me be afraid
> then of all such seeking the loves of the flesh. May
> I avoid it, pass it by. For the habit will form a
> character and the character a destiny. But the awful
> result is that one ceases to be conscious of the aw-
> fulness of sin: "After all this, you still say . . .
> 'I am innocent'" (Jer. 2:33–35).

In the following entry Tom mentions that he "played piano." Over the years, his habit after the morning service and after everyone had gone changed a bit. When we children were very young, he would often read to us. Jim remembers climbing onto his knee for the weekly ritual. When we were a little older, Tom often played the piano, frequently accompanied by the kids' singing, while Mum made dinner. After dinner Dad did the washing up while Mum went for a snooze; we kids might or might not help him, but it was not demanded. And after the dishes normally came family games before Dad slipped away to squeeze in a bit more preparation before the evening (French) service, but on this occasion he slipped out to visit some folk—on New Year's Day.

I cannot fail to mention that on one memorable occasion while I was still in high school, I went looking for Dad after the morning

service to entice him to come and play the piano while the rest of
us sang or played instruments. He was not where he usually was.
I found him in his study, the door not quite closed. He was on his
knees in front of his big chair, tears streaming down his face, as he
interceded with God for the handful of people to whom he had just
preached. I remember some of their names to this day.

Sunday, Jan. 1, 1961

The New Year has begun. Rose at 7:40. Dressed. Arranged Bible School supplies and Chapel, left in
disarray from watch night service. Bible School attendance 20; Morning Service . . . 16. Sermon: 1 Cor.
2:2—"A New Year's Resolve." At Communion service B.
served with me. [This "B." is one of the ones Tom had
mentioned in his 1959 journals as a nominal Christian who was being pursued by Jehovah's Witnesses.
Clearly his situation had improved. I remember him
and his wife as faithful and devout Christians before they moved away.] Asked Mr. O. to pray. Following the service I played piano. Dinner at 1:15.
Mother [Tom's mother, who by this time was a widow
and had a small apartment in Drummondville] stayed.
Then visited X.B. [Long list of friends and relatives
who were at X.B.'s house follows, including notes on
their spiritual condition.] But I have no fellowship any more with these who professed faith in the
Lord under my ministry. Seems evident they want to go
on—but no one has cared. . . . Father, forgive me.
Give them all back to Thee and to me. You know what
I mean, Father. Let me be faithful to Thee, and Thou
wilt help me to be zealous for others. . . . A heavy
snowstorm, and U. phoned through to say they were
caught in an accident at Roxton Falls. No one came
to the service. So the family visited the O.s. Sang
hymns. Pleasant evening. Home. Read Gen 1. Played
hymns. Bed at 12:25. Some prayer, some reading—but
how much was vital for God?

Sunday, Feb. 5, 1961

This morning I preached on Jairus: an anxious father,
a delaying Saviour, an earnest exhortation, a happy
outcome. In the evening I spoke from Acts 8:23 to
the end of the chapter, on Philip and the Ethiopian

eunuch. 20 present. 15 in the evening, 7 French Canadians. Visited Mother's afterward.

Monday, Feb. 6, 1961

Visited O.s in the evening. They lost their little
baby boy, stillborn, on Jan. 30. God has remarkably
sustained them in their loss, God giving them His
word and His grace. Sang hymns with them, read and
led in prayer. Visited B.s, where I met with them and
with two Catholics wearing a badge [in French], "I
BELIEVE. I am proud to be Catholic." "I BELIEVE" is a
monthly which "recalls you each month to the truths
of the Catholic faith learned at one time but so
easily forgotten." These gentlemen, Mr. Hot and Mr.
Beauchemin, were trying to win back the B.s to Ro-
manism. U. and his wife were also there. Mr. Hot was
quiet and well-spoken; Mr. Beauchemin, as also Mr. B.
and U., rather loud. Mr. B. is also ignorant. These
men are doing house-to-house visitation selling "I
BELIEVE" . . . and a calendar of Scripture readings.
Home at midnight.

Tuesday, Feb. 7, 1961

Prayed early, read late. In the afternoon I visited
Miss C. at the G.s. She professed to understand, but
it was clear that she did not. She promised to come
Sunday night. Then I visited Mr. Marcotte who is in
hospital for a few days. Spoke to a gentleman . . .
in the opposite bed. In the evening I visited B.s [an-
other "B."!], P.s, and Mr. G. Not much accomplished.

* Saturday, Feb. 25, 1961

This was a poor day . . . wasted in many respects.
Received a number of *Saturday Evening Posts* from the
Conyers [Tom's budget was so tight that he could not
subscribe to any of the standard journals and news
magazines, but certain families in the church passed
on their copies to Tom when they had finished with
them.] and read a number of articles. Help me, Lord,
to put away everything that does not contribute to
living for Jesus. Bed very late. There was a [French]
"Youth for Christ" meeting at Cap-de-la-Madeleine.
[One of the great challenges of the French works at
this stage was how to support and challenge the tiny

number of young people in each church. One of the
devices was to run "Youth for Christ" meetings once a
month at different regional centers, and people would
drive there across substantial distances—often fifty
or sixty miles.] I did not have the funds to pay gas,
so I was therefore relieved when the weather forecast
announced freezing rain. Joyce [by this time living in Montréal] went with Mme Frey [wife of William
Frey, the Swiss pastor who started working in French
Canada about the same time Tom did]. The place was
filled, I heard next day.

Sunday, Mar. 5, 1961

Rose 6:50 A.M. Prayer and study. Preached (poorly)
from 2 Cor. 2. Twenty-four present. . . . Rested.
Studied. Evening 19 present. Preached from Rom 1:1—17
(poorly). Saw Mr. F. to his home. Went to Mother's,
watched TV with her until 11:30, and was not edified.
Home. Went to bed reading my Bible. How much better
that is for my soul!

Sunday, Mar. 12, 1961

Rose 6:45 A.M. Preparations for Sunday School and
church. Preached on 2 Cor. 3:1—4. Fair time. Not
too many out: 20 present. Dinner. Sang around piano. Worked. Drove Joyce and Kay [her friend from
Montréal] to the bus [station for their intercity
coach back to Montréal]. Home. Rested. Arranged
chapel. Nineteen at French service. Preached same
sermon—more liberty. Drove folk home. Went to Mother's and watched TV with her [at this time we did
not have a TV ourselves]. Africa is emerging. Home.
Bed.

Sunday, May 28, 1961

Baccalaureate service at school. [There was a tradition of inviting a clergyman to speak briefly at
these services, and this was Tom's turn.] Subject:
Optima Petimus [Latin, "Let us seek the best"].

* Sunday, June 4, 1961

Just to note an undertaking . . . I shall let June
begin as the month of a book; the book will be 1 John.
My purpose: Read 1 John through once a day, reading

a different one of the following versions per day:
AV, Segond, ASV, Léger. Read one chapter per day in
Greek. Memorize a chapter in English, then in French,
and see what happens.

Tuesday, June 6, 1961

Another day when I've worked hard, especially on 1
John. But I've also addressed "Le Phare" [this small
Christian magazine was mailed out to many by using a
team of people to address individual copies, and Tom
was part of that team], visited Mr. G. and talked
with Mrs. G. I prepared a message for the young people: "The Challenge of Christ: The Challenge of His
Work, His Words, His Worth, and His Worship." . . . I
also spent hours on Wilson Ewin's book [Tom had been
asked to edit and polish it].

Thursday, June 8, 1961

I think it was Thursday last that Mrs. Donahue, the
mother of Mrs. G., died, and she was buried on Saturday. [Here explanation is required. Mrs. G. was
the wife of Dr. G., our family physician for about
ten years. He largely served the English-speaking
community and belonged to that vintage of doctors
who still made house calls. For ten years he visited our home when one of us kids was sick and was
able and helpful for all the regular things. This
care he lavished on us without asking for or receiv-
ing payment: he did this for all clergy. Four years
before this date, however, I had been sinking lower
and lower with some undiagnosed ailment. I was miss-
ing more than half my days at school. Eventually
Dr. G. told Dad and Mum to stop babying me: there was
nothing wrong with me. Still I sank lower, until my
parents brought me into Montréal to the specialists
of the Children's Hospital. After a week of tests, I
underwent major surgery that in fact saved my life.
Dr. G. did not really want to hear about it; my parents thereafter went to a younger and more up-to-
date French-speaking doctor. Dr. G., then, was the
man whose mother-in-law had just died.] Marg and I
considered the matter of sending a card and thought
we should try to do something concrete. She wanted
to offer her services to sit up with Mrs. G., herself dying of cancer. But we wondered whether a card

84   MEMOIRS OF AN ORDINARY PASTOR

would be resented, since . . . for several years he
has seemed to resent me. Alas! I ought to have sent
the card. Three-thirty Saturday morning I received a
telephone call from Dr. G. He had just brought his
wife into the hospital to die of cancer. "Are you a
parson? Are you a Christian? Mrs. G. has been wondering why nothing has come from the Carsons." I had
thought he might resent a card from me; now he was
furious that one had not been sent. So he proposed to
let every one of our people know of my perfidious-
ness. . . . This has cut deeply. He did not mention
that for the last four years, since we have gone to
another physician, there has been constraint [i.e.,
this was Tom's way of referring rather obliquely to
the awkwardness between the two families that made it
difficult to know how to respond]. . . . But surely,
O God, work in him and his wife as well as in me and
my family. Thou hast said, "Bless them that curse
you; if thine enemy hunger, feed him." Do Thou, then,
feed him. For Christ's sake. Amen.

* *Friday, June 16, 1961*
I prayed and was weighed down regarding Dr. and Mrs.
G. Telephoned him. She is very low in hospital. He
was quite kind over the telephone. It was God who did
it. Told Marg.

The journal entries all through this period hold many one-line
entries on family members. Many have the words "Talked with
Marg." When Tom came in from visitation in the afternoon, he and
Marg often disappeared into his study for half an hour, where they
talked through family matters, what had gone on in his visits, and
doubtless many more things that have not surfaced in the literary
remains. There are also entries like this one, dated Sunday, 2 July,
1961: "Last night started reading *Through Gates of Splendour* with
Marg." One-liners on his children also abound. One comments
rather acidly on a young man whom Joyce brought home for a visit.
About this time one finds, "Most of the afternoon was spent on
Don's cupboard"—surely one of the most opaque entries for those
who have no knowledge of our family. The basement had a couple
of old walk-in cupboards that had been used as root cellars for

storage or the like. At my urging, Dad converted one of them into a small lab, complete with good lighting, running water, a sink, a gas cylinder for a Bunsen burner, etc. I was beginning to take chemistry seriously. Tom spoke to our local pharmacist, and through him I managed to buy, from money saved from my after-school job at Canadian Tire, chemicals and in particular various reagents that simply do not come in ordinary chemistry sets (e.g., almost pure sulphuric acid). Five days later, "Had walk with Marg." Sometimes he took one of us on one of his trips: "Today Jimmie and I went to Ottawa. We drove the Lesages in to Montréal, and then we went on from there. . . . [We] went for a swim at Brighton Beach." A month later, "'Golfed' [i.e., miniature golf] with Jim."

In the recovery period after Jim's tonsillectomy, compounded with flu, "Jim beginning to seem somewhat better. Read books to him yesterday and today." The care for the family extended, of course, to looking after his own mother: "This day started on Mother's bedroom in the morning. Plastered. Bought paint. Gave ceiling one coat. . . . Joyce came home and slept at Grandma's. Bed at 12:45 A.M." Again: "Worked long hours on other things relating to Joyce's going away" (Joyce had quit her job in Montréal and had returned home long enough to pack up and move to Hamilton, Ontario, almost five hundred miles away, to begin nurses' training). In other words, whatever his own struggles, Tom was certainly not neglecting his own family. Moreover, after Joyce left home, Dad and Mum often had another young person living in the home, using her bedroom—usually a French-Canadian high-school student who lived with us while attending the English high school so as to become bilingual.

His own tendency to blame himself for everything during this period made it especially difficult for him to understand his kids when they were trying to shift the blame to someone else:

* *Sunday, Aug. 27, 1961*
Rose 7:30. Prayer of confession and worship. Read 1 Cor. 15–16. Prepared for services. Fifteen at Sunday School, nineteen at morning service. Preached poorly as I had not adequately prepared. Had a good

```
outline; discouraged but not in despair. Read Gen 5—8
and Ps 73—74. Dinner. Joyce's record was broken, but
why did not Don take the blame? I feel discouraged,
for both these children are so dear to me, both want
to go on with God, but the unwillingness to credit
the possibility of being at fault—this baffles me.
```

Shifting blame from himself was something Tom never did. If he felt he had been unfair with any of his children, he was the first to confess it. In September 1961, for instance, we drove to Hamilton to drop Joyce off at her nursing school and stopped in Toronto for the wedding of a niece (Gail Carson, the older daughter of Tom's brother Reg). Tom comments, "Very nice. I was a poor toastmaster—and how I felt I had spoiled some of it. Drove to Reg's, thence to Hamilton. Because of being so depressed because of failure I was too strict on Joyce's driving. Changed [drivers—i.e., back to himself!] at Oakville. It upset all of us. Went for a long walk for an hour. Home and to bed. How I need God!" But, of course, it could not rest there. The next day's entry begins, "Up fairly early. Prayer, cried for help. Picked up Joyce and we went to Westside [Baptist Church] Sunday School and morning service. Things corrected."

Often there are brief entries on what he was reading. The range of such reading is commendable, granted that his Bible reading came first and that his reading spanned books in English and in French. In August 1961, for instance, he was reading *Philosophie de l'esprit*, plus *Annals of Christian Martyrdom*, while working on his Hebrew. Occasionally in the evening he indulged in the newspaper's crossword puzzle. The next month he was reading J. Gresham Machen's *What Is Faith?* and enjoying it hugely, along with one of the books of Jacques Maritain, *Réflexions sur l'Amérique*; the next month, a book on homiletics and another on the Dead Sea Scrolls, while re-reading something of James Stalker that he had first read while at seminary. Sporadically over the years he returned to certain standard works such as Spurgeon's *An All-Round Ministry*.

Interspersed with these generally mundane but faithful entries, however, are the occasional entries that show Tom sliding into the slough of despond. The most detailed and excruciating of these is

found in mid-October 1961. Even now, I am not sure that it would
be wise to publish the whole of it. The gist of it, however, is easily
summarized, and some of it I shall quote:

Tom begins:

> First, a word or two on my prayer of this morning.
> I confessed to God the sins of cowardice and lazi-
> ness. Yesterday morning, perhaps because I blamed my
> long stretch of driving for a weariness which I was
> bound to have [five hundred miles without interstate
> highways]—it is so easy to do, it has been so easy
> to do all along—I picked up a . . . novel and read
> it through. Oh, I do not do this often, but how many
> not only profitable, but useful works are neglected
> in favour of such so-called "recreation." Anyway,
> all these things are getting me down. And this morn-
> ing, without more ado, I have confessed the real
> sins of my life to God, laziness and cowardice. "You
> wicked and slothful servant." . . . That wicked ser-
> vant said, "I was afraid, and hid the talent in the
> earth." The Lord would have none of it: "wicked and
> slothful" was what he said.

Tom goes on to survey his life through stunningly negative fil-
ters. He recalls how hard and honorably he worked before he went
to seminary, when his employer was Metropolitan Life, but since
then, he avers, he has simply not been as faithful. At seminary, he
claims, he did not work as hard as he might have, partly because he
broke up with a young woman and was badly distracted emotion-
ally. He never finished his degree program at seminary: in those days,
it required a thesis, and this he never finished. (This thesis needed
to be only about sixty pages. He chose to write on the theological
tendencies and aberrations of Horace Bushnell. I have beside me as
I write about two hundred pages of his notes, about a third handwritten, two-thirds typed, single space.) He never finished, he says,
because he had very little income apart from what he earned from
teaching piano, he was spending too much time with Marg, and he
generally felt a failure. When he accepted the call to Emmanuel, he
began with enthusiasm, but he felt he did not do well there either, so
he resigned, giving the reason that he felt called to the French work.

He did learn French pretty well in the years 1943–1947 while he was on Union salary. "But I was not a genuine dedicated missionary after souls. I tried, but power was lacking. Only a very few came to the Lord, oh, so few."

He acknowledges that when he went to Drummondville, he thought that might centralize his work. "And I finally felt, though at first I had not, that here God wanted me. I came, stayed in circumstances that severely tried me and many. Dr. Shields commented that what I wanted was a nice home! Sometimes I wonder, O God, 'vile and full of sin I am!'" His assessment of these Drummondville years is just as bleak: "But I have accomplished nothing. I had not the missionary spirit, nor the evangelist's passion." He then proceeds to list the numbers of homes he has not yet visited.

So what is to be gained from fresh resolutions to be more consistent? Nothing! But what else is he to do but plead for grace and carry on? A few days later he writes, "I am discouraged, but I am trying to put quitting entirely out of my mind."

Yet it would be totally unrealistic to think that all of Tom's reflections were so negative. These more extreme episodes are not typical. Only a few weeks later, for instance, we read entries like this:

* *Sunday, Dec. 10, 1961*
Rose 7:00 A.M., dressed, prayer, very conscious of my great need of God. So little time properly to prepare, but God is with me. "Nothing in my hands I bring, / Simply to thy cross I cling." Sunday School: "Sin and the Blood," Heb. 9:22. Morning service: Preached strongly, I believe with God's help, but not a sermon thoroughly prepared. Lord, help me to continue. . . . [After evening service, he drove some folks home.] Home myself, a fair day. Sunday School was down, about 15. Morning service, 20; evening service, 22.

* *Saturday, Dec. 16, 1961*
Rose 5:45 A.M., Bible, prayer, other reading. Did clean chapel. . . . Took Don skating, picked him up after. He is a good lad. So is Jimmie. Thank God for

my (our) children, so well taught by Marg. [This is
a fascinating entry. Mum so often taught us wisdom,
as I recall it, but Dad taught us a great deal of the
Bible and theology, helping us to distinguish between
orthodoxy and unorthodoxy, giving us things to read
and reflect on, forcing us to debate him on, say,
Catholic theology.]

The year 1962 brought much more of the same. Entries brought lists of things done (from shoveling snow to visiting recalcitrant alcoholics, from sermon preparation to Tom's own spiritual exercises), and some moments of bleakness. In January 1962 Tom stumbled across the sentence from Spurgeon in *An All-Round Ministry*: "I may not judge, but sometimes think that when brethren bring the converts in so slowly, they have a trembling about the power of saving grace to bear so many." "Perhaps," Tom comments, "but more, they have not had victory in their own lives."

Meanwhile, I had succumbed to a severe case of Osgood-Schlatter's disease in both knees and was in a lot of pain. Tom's entry for Monday, January 15, 1962, includes the lines, "Drove children to school, home, a weeping heart over Don. How he suffers! O God, you know why. . . . Then I began wondering what I had said yesterday which could in any way have helped Don. I remembered nothing." In those days the treatment called for full casts on both legs, so that is what I was eventually given, which took me out of sports for more than a year.

In February there is a slightly amusing entry—amusing in retrospect—that reflects another small crisis that was developing in the home, this one centered around Tom's rather naive generosity. He kept the family books but was so generous with household money that sometimes Marg was almost desperate as to how to make ends meet by the end of each fiscal month. "Tried to put all my monies right and go out and bring Marg up-to-date. For some reason things went wrong. She seemed to accuse me of handing out money to every Tom, Dick, and Harry. When I suggested I keep a record so she could see what I did with the money, she became very upset— why, I do not know. I meant no harm, though she took it that way."

After a few more confrontations, Marg, with Tom's agreement, took over the family finances. There was never any hesitation about tithing and other gifts, but once Marg controlled the purse strings, Tom was given a limited budget for car expenses and the like and whatever additional acts of charity he wished to undertake. But if he ran out of money before the end of the month, it came out of the gas money, not the food money. The problem was resolved. Tom did not control the family finances again until Marg started to sink into Alzheimer's.

In the early autumn of 1962 there are oblique references in Tom's journals to long conversations he is having with Marg, and eventually reaching a firm decision. His journals do not at that point tell us what it is to which he is referring. In fact, together they swore a solemn vow before the Lord, a vow of which his journals do not speak for another year—certainly a vow of which no one in the church or family was aware. For the previous year, from the autumn of 1961 until the autumn of 1962, there had not been a single conversion. Together Tom and Marg resolved to seek the face of God in intercession and renewed commitment to the work for one more year; but if by the autumn of 1963 there had not been any conversions and other signs of grace, Tom would resign from the work in Drummondville.

Entries in Tom's journals reflect something of his ongoing personal ups and downs, but there is, I think, less desperation: a course had been charted. Each Sunday is carefully recorded: e.g., Sunday, January 6, 1963, English 25, French 23. There is the usual round of physical chores: snow shoveling ("Don and I cleaned the entrance tonight," Saturday, February 2), cleaning the chapel, keeping the car running, and the like, and the long lists of people he was visiting, triumphs and failures in the lives of his little flock, sermons he was preparing and preaching—and occasional days of despair.

That was my last Spring at home: I was about to graduate from high school. There is a slightly painful entry dated Saturday, May 18, 1963. Dad and Mum drove me and another high school student, a lass called Christina Martha, into Montréal so we could take some entrance exams at McGill University. Dad faithfully records that

both Chris and I paid $1.50 for tickets for something or other—he
doesn't say what, and I cannot recall—and adds, "We wished we
could afford to pay for them." Tom was busy not only with his
regular rounds of ministry but was preparing some radio addresses
for a program that Ernie Keefe—one of the "jailbirds"!—had managed to secure on a station thirty miles away. The entry for Saturday,
June 29, 1963, includes the line, "Took a walk with Marg last night,
spoke more of possibility of leaving Drummondville." That summer Tom also attempted some open-air meetings, which garnered
some interest but no conversions. Toward the end of the summer
he learned that one of the crucial families in the French congregation was moving away from the area. In September I went off to
McGill on a full-ride scholarship. During my first year at university,
Dad and Mum would scrimp and save and send me a total of ten
dollars. And that October, 1963, one month after I left home, Tom
announced his resignation to the church in Drummondville.

It came as a complete surprise. The minutes of the church meeting for October 6, 1963, record pages of discussion, trying to find
ways to induce Tom to stay on, raising the possibility of not accept-
ing his resignation, wondering if steps might be taken to encourage
him, and so forth. Tom had offered to continue preaching for some
months while another pastor was sought, and some wondered if
that arrangement could be extended indefinitely. Tom told them of
his solemn vow, taken one year previously. Finally one wise woman,
Mrs. Millar, "stated that it was obvious from the Pastor's . . . letter
that he was decided in his mind to make this change and that we
should accept his resignation and put ourselves immediately into
the hands of the Fellowship in order that the Lord's work might be
continued in Drummondville."

Tom was fifty-two.

Most certainly he did not see himself retreating from ministry.

Granted the purpose of this volume, I think it wise to pause
here and reflect a little on the discouraging face of this chapter. The
longer I have spent getting to know pastors in many small and medi-
um-size churches (and some larger ones!), the more I have become
aware of the chasms of discouragement through which many of

them pass. The reasons for such discouragement are many, but some of them, at least, overlap with Tom's self-doubt, guilty conscience, sense of failure, long hours, and growing frustration with apparent fruitlessness. Some reflection on these matters some four and a half decades after the events will not only put some of Tom's comments into perspective but may help discouraged ministers of the gospel today.

(1) Dad had a view of work that sprang in part from the Great Depression: anything less than working all the time was letting down the people and the Lord. There is no hint in his journals or letters of the proper place of rest, of pacing himself, of Jesus' words, "Come with me by yourselves to a quiet place and get some rest" (Mark 6:31, NIV). In Dad this was married to a bit of a perfectionist streak. That, I suspect, played a big part in his failure to finish his thesis: the work was never good enough, so it was never complete. And the sense of failure from not completing it added to the pattern of failure, which in turn engendered more defeat.

I do not wish to make excuses for Dad. Certainly I am not in a position to judge him. But there are gospel ways of tackling this problem more hopefully. So many aspects of ministry demand excellence, and there are not enough hours in the day to be excellent in all of them. When I was a young man, I heard D. Martyn Lloyd-Jones comment that he would not go across the street to hear himself preach. Now that I am close to the age he was when I heard him, I am beginning to understand. It is rare for me to finish a sermon without feeling somewhere between slightly discouraged and moderately depressed that I have not preached with more unction, that I have not articulated these glorious truths more powerfully and with greater insight, and so forth. But I cannot allow that to drive me to despair; rather, it must drive me to a greater grasp of the simple and profound truth that we preach and visit and serve under the gospel of grace, and God accepts us because of his Son. I must learn to accept myself not because of my putative successes but because of the merits of God's Son. The ministry is so open-ended that one *never* feels that all possible work has been done, or done as well as one might like. There are always more people to visit, more studying to be done, more preparation to do. What Christians must do, what Christian *leaders* must do, is constantly remember that we serve our God and Maker and Redeemer under the gospel of grace. Dad's diaries show he understood this truth in theory, and sometimes he exulted in it (as when he was reading Machen's *What Is Faith?*), but quite frankly, his sense of failure sometimes blinded him to the glory of gospel freedom.

(2) Mum used to tell us kids, "Work hard, and play hard, but never confuse the two." By this she wanted us to know that while we were working, we should not fritter away the hours by squeezing in distractions and various kinds of play. The result would be poor work combined with guilt feelings for a job poorly done. Similarly, when we were playing we were not supposed to be thinking about work because that would dilute some of the regenerative value of downtime. But Dad never learned Mum's simple maxim. The total number of hours he put into his calling each week was excessively high, but occasionally—as much out of fatigue as discouragement—he would permit something else to intrude, and then feel guilty about it. Mum's maxim should be posted on the mirrors of most ministers.

(3) It is always disconcerting to see other ministers *in your own sphere of service* working effectively and fruitfully while you are plagued with stagnation. When that happens, there may be things to learn from more fruitful ministries, but sometimes one must simply rejoice that some ministers are more fruitful and more blessed than you are, thereby learning to rejoice with those who rejoice. Tom was singularly free of the green-eyed monster. Insofar as he reflected on the relative successes of others, he did not envy them or make excuses for himself; rather, he took it as evidence that his dark self-assessment was correct. Yet in many respects this self-reproach was unrealistic. Most of the French works in Québec at this time were stalled. A strong work might climb to thirty or forty people but usually did not stay there very long. Almost ten more years would pass before there was a dramatic improvement. During the fifties and sixties, French-speaking churches did not ever grow by having the right programs and promotions. This was

still slogging work in a fairly hostile environment. Even a few years later, in 1969, when I started working with Bill Phillips to plant a church in Ahuntsic (an area of about 125,000 people in Montréal), I visited about three thousand homes before I got the first Bible study going. That was simply the way it was. By this juncture, however, Tom was burning out. Fewer were being converted than in his early days in Montréal.

(4) Tom had a remarkably tender conscience. On so many fronts this is a good thing. Indeed, in the Christian way it is an almost universally recognized truth that the closer a believer is to God, the more deeply he or she recognizes and feels the weight of personal sin. This might become an insupportable burden if it is not joined with an ever-deepening grasp of the limitless dimensions of the love of God (cf. Ephesians 3:14–21). In Tom's case, he not only felt his own sin, but the failures and sins of those in his con-gregations, English or French, he charged to his own failures as a pastor. Perhaps some were his fault, but certainly not all: Jesus had his Judas, Paul his Demas. Tom was developing a glass-half-empty analysis of himself that was not, finally, realistic. It was certainly not in line with what his parishioners, his colleagues in ministry, or his own family members thought of him.

(5) To his enormous credit and his family's good, at no point did he ignore his wife and children. All of us look back on ways we might have acted better or more wisely with respect to our own families, and inevitably we become conscious of the grace of God in our lives. But Tom did not fall into the assorted temptations that sometimes detach a minister from his family or even lead him to betray them.

(6) I have already mentioned that what seemed to Dad an advan-tage at the beginning of the Drummondville work—that it would be bilingual—eventually proved a serious disadvantage. Other communities had followed the Drummondville pattern: Sept-Iles, Noranda, Val d'Or, Malartic, Hull, Maniwaki, Valleyfield. The logic in favor of the arrangement seemed inescapable. The rela-tively small English-speaking communities were getting a pastor they could not otherwise afford, while pledging themselves, with

mission help from the Fellowship, to support outreach into the French-speaking population of their communities. Unfortunately, however, "the law of unintended consequences" soon kicked in. Support from the English side meant that there was less pressure on the French side to become independent. The francophone congregations always felt like the junior sibling. Development of French-speaking leadership was slower: let the English do it, for they already know what they are doing. Equally detrimental, the bilingual pastors were pouring their energies into two congregations with two languages, two cultures, two sets of friends, two sets of associations, two educational systems, and so forth. Neither job was done very well: there simply were not enough hours in the day. The first to realize this was Murray Heron up in Noranda: about 1960 or thereabouts he withdrew from the English side and devoted himself exclusively to the French side. He was soon followed by his brother Lorne in Val d'Or and Malartic. Tom was on the slow end of perceiving the need for this change. Indeed, his successor in Drummondville, Pastor Y. Hurtubise, soon analyzed the problem and successfully led the church in this direction, and within ten years all the remaining bilingual works became unilingual French-language churches.

(7) Much Christian contentment turns on perceiving things in the right grid. In his journals Tom could cite Paul's words in Philippians 4 about the apostle's contentment irrespective of circumstances and Nehemiah's insistence that the joy of the Lord is our strength (Nehemiah 8:10) and take comfort and delight from them. Precisely how, then, do such passages become integrated with others that reflect the most profound self-abasement and contrition? It is relatively easy to develop a formulaic framework for the integration of such complementary stances, but it is infinitely more complex to work them out in the hurly-burly of an individual life.

(8) Time would disclose another factor to be carefully evaluated. Tom worked best on a team on which others were ordering his life and work for him, and he was set free to play to his strengths. Of course, that was not possible in Drummondville; it is not possible in many small churches today. Self-knowledge, however, is vital, and in

the next chapter and beyond we shall see how this self-knowledge eventually was forced on Tom's mind.

(9) We should recognize that Tom's journal entries expressing deepest anguish frequently have the texture of biblical lament. Tom never stands in judgment of God; he never curses God. In his gloomiest moments Tom ends up with a cry for help.

CHAPTER SEVEN

CIVIL SERVANT AND
MINISTER OF THE GOSPEL

$\mathcal{D}$oubtless Tom saw his resignation from Faith Baptist Church / Église Baptiste de la Foi in Drummondville as the fulfillment of a vow rightly made in good conscience before the living God. But how would he support his family? Tom and Marg had no savings, almost no retirement benefits, and no house. One of the biblical passages that burned in Tom's conscience as the deadline of his vow loomed larger on the horizon was 1 Timothy 5:8: "But if any provide not for his own, and specially for those of his own house, he hath denied the faith, and is worse than an infidel."

Tom knew that he would immediately receive invitations from anglophone churches in the Fellowship, but as far as he was concerned that was simply not an option. He was called to French Canada and would not leave Québec. None of the twenty or so French-language Fellowship churches was open at the moment. And he frankly had no energy or drive to try to begin a new work elsewhere, even if he could persuade the Fellowship French Board to fund him.

While hunting around for suitable employment, Tom stumbled across a newspaper advertisement for a competition for a job with the federal government as a French/English translator. He was told he could bring a dictionary; so true to his nature he brought along an unobtrusive pocket French/English dictionary. When he arrived in

Ottawa for the test, he was startled by the number of people apply-
ing and dismayed to see that all of them had brought large reference
dictionaries. He thought that, humanly speaking, his chances at this
post were shot. As it turned out, he achieved the highest grade—so
high, in fact, that the examiners upgraded his rank and salary before
his first day of work. Inevitably Tom saw this as gracious confirma-
tion from God's providential hand that this really was the move he
should make. In fact, Tom's perfectionist streak, his love of detail,
and his "faithful to the text" training exactly suited the demands of
the new job. Despite his age, he soon became a reviser of translation
and then a highly respected reviser of revisers.[1]

So Tom remained with the Canadian Civil Service until the
mandatory retirement age. He did not see himself as abandoning
the ministry, still less the French work; rather, he saw himself as a
"tent-making" pastor. Tom's years with the Civil Service had many
effects, some of them the results of his own decisions, some of them
thrust upon him.

First, his new job was in Ottawa, but Tom and Marg decided to
make their home across the Ottawa River in Québec, on the French
side, in the almost entirely French-speaking city of Hull. Here there
was another small bilingual Fellowship Baptist church—Montclair
Baptist Church / Église Baptiste Montclair. Its pastor was Wilf
Wellington, one of the two men who had started in Québec about
the same time Tom did. Wilf and his wife Edna had no children
and had devoted themselves to Québec over the decades without
hesitation or reserve. His French was still rough and would be until
he died, but he had the commitment to the gospel and to French
Canada that characterized all the early workers. He soon had Tom
serving in the Montclair church in many ways, as we shall see.

Second, Tom's move away from Drummondville started an
unintended chain reaction among the francophone churches. This
generated several small victories: several pastors took on fresh life

---

[1]Perhaps it is worth mentioning that all this translation work was French to English; he never
passed the English to French exams. The standards of the Canadian government in translation are
extraordinarily high, and it is very rare that any translator is competent enough to translate *out* of
his or her mother tongue rather than *into* it. By this stage Tom's French was punctiliously correct
but sometimes still lacked the idiomatic fluency of someone brought up in the language.

as they moved from the positions in which they had been stalled. This may not be an ideal development, but in the Lord's providence this is what happened.

Third, when Tom and Marg first moved to Hull, they settled into a small upstairs flat with their remaining son Jim, who still had three more years of high school to go. Mum returned to nursing— more precisely, she found work as a nursing aide, as her credentials were substantially out-of-date. With two incomes and considerable frugality, Tom and Marg managed, one year later, to get a mortgage on an adequate house in Hull, a mortgage they could pay off by the time Tom retired from the Civil Service. Worry over finances simply does not surface in Tom's journals, but this must have been something of a relief nevertheless.

Fourth, Tom's work for the government was the sort of thing he tackled with energy for the requisite number of hours and then could leave behind him when he came home. The work of the ministry is *never* like that. This not only provided Tom with a release from stress but still gave him evening and weekend hours to continue his pastoral ministry.

Fifth, Tom's journals show that he had no sooner started work as a translator than he was praying for and talking with colleagues at work about the gospel and berating himself for not being a better evangelist.

There were two dark sides to this transition. While some of Tom's fellow pastors wrote to him with kind words of encouragement, a few either berated him or ignored him as something of a slightly embarrassing failure. At Montclair, Wilf Wellington certainly needed help: the numbers were not much greater than in Drummondville, but bilingual churches present many draining challenges. Moreover, at this juncture Wellington himself was often away on Fellowship business. Tom found himself preaching regularly, not only at Montclair but elsewhere, and with growing lists of people to visit and care for. Wellington himself kept suggesting, not only in private but sometimes in front of Marg and Jim, that Tom should return to "full-time ministry" as soon as possible.

That in turn led to the second dark side in this transition. Even in his last year or two in Drummondville, Tom was beginning to face health problems, doubtless springing as much from stress as from anything else. The pressures on Tom both from external counsel and from his own desire to be as useful as possible led to serious collapse. In the course of the next few years he twice landed in the hospital, once near death, with exhaustion, heart problems, and blood clots. At the Christmas break in 1965, while I was in my third year at McGill, I brought home a Muslim friend who had no place else to go for the break when the dorms were shut down. The first night we were home, an ambulance arrived in the middle of the night to transport Dad to the hospital, and he remained there until after Mohammed Yusuf Guraya and I had left to return to university. After the second of these episodes, Pastor Wellington, perhaps feeling a little guilty at the pressure he had been imposing, asked Jim if he thought that he, Wellington, had been pushing Tom too hard. Jim simply answered, "Yes." There was less pressure after that.

But Tom was also getting his own act together a little better. There was a swimming pool to which Civil Servants had free access, and several times a week Tom started swimming laps during his lunch break. In the winter he would use the same block of time to skate for miles on the frozen Rideau Canal. Tom's journals, not so regularly written during this period, begin to reflect a lighter tone. Throughout the years those journals always maintain a certain level of introspection, self-examination, and contrition, but they begin to sound less desperate, more confident in the sheer grace of God. Sometimes, too, denominational and other Christian leaders were turning to Tom for accurate translation of materials that needed to be in both languages, which, of course, was work he not only handled well but thoroughly enjoyed.

There is a slightly amusing record in the church minutes at Montclair in mid-1964, about nine months after Tom and Marg arrived in Hull. A motion was made to ask Mr. Carson to be assistant pastor of the church. "He himself," the record states, "expressed his desire to remain as one in the pew rather than as a leader, but would do whatever the church thought necessary in the work." The discussion developed along various lines, and the tasks of the potential assistant pastor were outlined:

> . . . from time to time to replace Mr. Wellington in his absence (he of necessity has to be away sometimes because of the general needs of the French work), discuss matters with the deacons, counsel on visitation, take young Christians with him on visits that they may learn from him, taking the adult class in Mr. Wellington's absence, and also the 11:00 a.m. service and evening service; for in a bilingual church the work is almost doubled.

Mrs. Wellington then "remarked that Mr. Carson was already doing all this." The motion carried, simply to give recognition to what was already being done. There was, of course, no remuneration.

Interesting journal entries during this period include the following (about half of them now in French):

Tuesday, Jan. 21, 1964

"Greatness is not a matter of a lofty position and exercise of authority, but of service" (John Balyo). . . . Let me take this to heart.

Wednesday, June 24, 1964

Bought and paid for and cut up forty pieces of wood for Marg for her DVBS [Daily Vacation Bible School] class. My commitments:

```
Read: Greek
Do: Translation
Read: Books
Write: Letters
Send: cheque
Prepare: for boys
Send: money to Frey
```

Monday, Aug. 3, 1964

A blessed half hour of prayer.

Tuesday, Dec. 22, 1964

7:45 A.M.: Theme for 1965: "Ye that are the Lord's remembrancers, take ye no rest, and give him no rest,

till he establish, and till he make Jerusalem a
praise in the earth" (Isa. 61:6, 7 [*sic;* the reference is really 62:6—7]).

In February 1965 Tom is still setting himself impossible goals
and then berating himself for failing to meet them:

Tuesday, Feb. 9, 1965

In prayer I have set myself, as Assistant Pastor of
Montclair, a goal of ten hours per week on church
work, apart from preaching and teaching. I worked it
out this way: Mon, 2 hours; Tues, 2 hours; Wed, zero
[because that was prayer meeting night, and he was
at church anyway, often speaking!]; Thurs, 2 hours;
Sat morning, 4 hours. . . . This does not include
private devotions. [Friday is also omitted because
on that night, by this time, Tom was sponsoring the
young people's group.]

Saturday, July 24, 1965

My immediate reason for writing is to note one or
two points from Joshua, for I have continued reading
consecutively. However, I should note that there have
been real encouragements at the Montclair Church, and
I am sure there would be many more if I was not such
a dead weight and a drag. [He then lists a couple recently baptized and three adult professions of faith.
This is followed by some reflective meditations on
Joshua.] I finally, this evening, confessed my sin
and got to work somewhat. It seems so utterly hypo-
critical to go on as though no sin has been committed
without some kind of penance, but God says there is
only one penance—Jesus' sacrifice on Calvary, Jesus'
blood. I plead it and go on, knowing that I shall
fall again.

Monday, Sept. 26, 1965

Yesterday I was so privileged to listen to that
saintly man of God, Wilfrid Wellington, in the morning: "Godliness with contentment is great gain."

On 16 June 1966, Tom's mother, who had moved back to
the Ottawa area when they did, "went home at 6:00 P.M." and

was buried two days afterward. Tom comments two weeks later: "She was all a mother should be, and it is a regret to me that I did not do all that I might have to make her happy. But I loved her, and we shall see her again on that bright morning. And never a daughter was more devoted to her than was my wife."

In the Spring of 1967, when the numbers at Montclair were roughly what they had been in Drummondville four years earlier, Pastor Wilf Wellington resigned. He himself had succumbed to discouragement. The minutes of the church tell us that the leaders asked Tom if he would succeed Wilf as pastor. He took two weeks to think and pray about the decision and offered an alternative proposal: he would take on most of the pastoral responsibilities for one year, without remuneration, while maintaining his Civil Service job to enable the small church to clear a debt that was weighing on it. This ministry commitment included preaching four times most Sundays. Marg quit her own nursing job so she could carry more of the load at home, including handling more of the phone calls. A year and a half later, Tom indicated that he was willing to continue helping out in this way until a new pastor arrived but was not willing to take the post "full-time" himself. During this period he was so busy he left no journal entries. Nevertheless both the English and the French sides grew somewhat and stabilized.

In 1971 the church called a young man who was woefully unsuited to the post and left two years later. For those two years, Tom's duties in the church were mercifully reduced, and by 1972 he again started keeping his journal sporadically. As usual, many of the entries simply report the events of the day, those coming to him for premarital counseling, special prayer requests, and the like. But some are more interesting.

*Friday, June 30, 1972

Talked with Marg re Don's prospects for going for his Ph.D. [At this point I was pastor of a church in Vancouver and in the throes of deciding whether or

not to resign and pursue doctoral study in England.]
Wrote up diary. No really wasted time so far.

Pleasant lunch with my wife. . . . Some reading today in Whitefield and David Brainerd. In that regard
a fairly good day.

Monday, July 3, 1972

Afternoon not much; in the evening we went to Com-
edy at the Arts Centre, tickets provided by Jim.
[At this point Jim was the assistant to the director of the National Arts Centre in Ottawa.] Singing
magnificent; plot, featuring unfaithfulness—well, it
depressed me that I was there. Home. Bed.

Wednesday, Oct. 4, 1972

Don took the plane at Ottawa Airport at 7:30 P.M. for
Montréal, and at 9:30 P.M. for London. We did not have
much prayer together; we did have good fellowship in
many ways with consciousness of the Lord. O God, may
he walk with Thee.

On the weekend of 6–8 October, Tom mentions that Jim
has returned home from seminary: Jim had started as a student
at Central Baptist Seminary that autumn. This time he brought
Lois Hartwig home with him, his girlfriend and future wife. But
there is also mention of the "Brookdale Annual Meeting." Tom
had agreed to serve on the board of the Brookdale Farm, an
orphanage with Christian roots about an hour away by car. He
served on this board until he died, and for him this was a commitment that sometimes involved quite a lot of work. Shortly
thereafter he also became treasurer of another small mission,
a responsibility he diligently discharged until the last weeks of
his life.

On 5 January 1973, Tom rejoices that Joyce and her husband
and two daughters have just returned safely from about four years
in Papua New Guinea, then adds, "My foot is acting up." This was
one of several traumas over blood clots. The next day was Marg's
birthday, and he was in too much pain to take her out. The next

day, Sunday, he nevertheless dragged himself to church to play the organ, then staggered home to bed.

Sunday, Feb. 4, 1973

Preached at Lachute, morning and evening, and at Dalesville in the afternoon. More at Lachute in the morning; Dalesville fewer. . . . Home safe, in the mercy of God, for ten to twenty miles were exceedingly slippery [he drove home in a snowstorm]. Thanked the Lord for being present. I had prayed, "If thou goest not with me, carry me not up hence."

The Montclair church was beginning to slide. The young man who was the pastor was constantly whipping the people. Still worse, from Tom's perspective, was his mishandling of the Word of God. Tom's style was to be astonishingly non-confrontational about most things, but any serious mishandling of Scripture would almost always spur him to confront the individual. Hence:

Sunday, Mar. 18, 1973

Very distressed at the message this morning. The text was 1 P. 5. The pastor was "expounding" "God resisteth the proud," and he used Joseph as an illustration, picturing him as being very full of pride such that it finally brought him to all the troubles of Egypt. I was so shocked I said to him on the way out, "You have slandered one of the saintliest characters in the Bible." We had a talk this P.M., and I asked him if he had considered that he was not called to the pastorate; I also mentioned other matters.

Sunday, Mar. 25, 1973

The pastor again preached from 1 P. 5, this time about resisting the devil. His message was sober, good, but missed the text. He took "stablish" to mean "re-establish," and talked mainly of Peter's denial and later confession, and said the Lord was willing to re-establish backsliding Christians as He said in this text. The message was true, but had nothing to do with the text.

Sunday, April 1, 1973

The pastor preached from Phil 1:6 and (principally)
from Phil 3, but got loving each other out of it.
We should love each other, but the text is speaking
of reaching for "the excellency of the knowledge of
Christ Jesus my Lord."

Saturday, April 7, 1973

Spent several hours translating latest documents for
Brookdale. Watched last period of hockey game between
Canadiens and Buffalo Sabres. Canadiens won 5-2, but
Buffalo had forty-four shots on goal to Canadiens'
twenty-seven. A pretty good day, but I'm not on the
ball for my Lord. How different my diary is from that
of David Brainerd.

By July the numbers in the church had gone down dramatically. According to the church minutes of 18 July 1973, the
pastor announced that he was resigning, effective 2 September
1973. He said that the finances were becoming too difficult, but
that above all he thought the "main problem" was "our spiritual
standing as a church," and announced a day of prayer for 27
July. Astonishingly, the pastor then asked "Mr. Carson" to speak
up and say what he thought. The minutes record, "Mr. Carson
then pointed out to the pastor that the people needed to be fed
from the Word, not scolded."

Tom was about to become the interim pastor once again.

Thursday, Sept. 6, 1973.

    6:40 A.M. I'd rather have Jesus than silver or
gold;
    I'd rather have Him than have riches untold.
    I'd rather have Jesus than houses or lands;
    I'd rather be led by his nail-pierced hands—
    Than to be the king of a vast domain
    And be held in sin's dread sway.
    I'd rather have Jesus than anything
    This world affords today.

    One thought in prayer, and I hasten to record it.
Jesus said, "Come ye after me, and I will make you

to become fishers of men" (Mark 1:17). Cf. Mt. 4:17
[sic; actually 4:19], Lu. 5:10 and Jo. 1:35—44 and
following. Read several chapters in Proverbs. Translated letters for Deacons' Meeting.

*Monday, Nov. 19, 1973

[Re a woman who is deeply troubled as to whether or
not she is saved]: She does not know how to lay her
worries on the Lord. Oh, may I learn how to pray for
her. I spent an hour with L. She sees [her husband]
M. leaving. I strongly drew her attention to 1 Peter 3:1—6. O God, help her to do your will. May she
not give in to the old nature as her way to respond.
Perform, O Lord, a miracle in her life. And bless
the church.

Today I prayed at length that the Lord would help
me to become a soul-winner. I told him, in effect,
that I would prefer to be able to talk about Jesus in
order to attract men and women to him than any other
thing. But I know I am fearful.

Tuesday, Nov. 20, 1973

Today the Lord answered my prayer. Mrs. L. [a lady at
his Civil Service job, not the "L" mentioned in the
previous entry] came by to say a simple hello. She
had been absent for three days owing to the death of
her aunt, who died at age eighty-five. In the course
of the conversation she casually mentioned that she
hoped everyone would go to heaven when they died. I
told her of the two ways Jesus talks about, one leading to perdition. And then I preached Christ. At the
end I suddenly realized that God was giving me an
opportunity to become a soul-winner.

This evening P.L. phoned with some questions. . . .
[At the end of the conversation] I gave her the hours
of our services for her and her household. O God, you
are so good to me.

Tom did not yet know how good. The wind of the Spirit had
begun to blow through Québec.

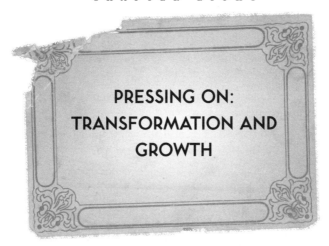

CHAPTER EIGHT

PRESSING ON: TRANSFORMATION AND GROWTH

*T*he "Quiet Revolution" had passed through Québec, and in its wake most of its citizens, especially its younger citizens, were much less tightly tied to the Roman Catholic Church. Yet this had also fomented a spiritual hunger. Moreover, political changes had begun to transform the education systems—changes described in the first chapter of this book. Even within the Catholic Church, the impact of Vatican II was deeply troubling Québec citizens.[1] Before Vatican II, it would have been difficult to find a single vehicle driven by a French-Canadian that did not have a St. Christopher medal hanging from the rearview mirror. Vatican II "de-sainted" Christopher and many other saints, and at the popular level the shock could be felt across the Province. Perhaps the Catholic Church was not stable and trustworthy after all.

God raised up a handful of remarkable leaders. The most remarkable was doubtless Jacques Alexanian. As a lad, his father Pascal had barely and dramatically escaped the slaughter of the Armenians by the Turks—the first, but certainly not the last, genocide of the twentieth century. After knocking around the Middle East, Pascal eventually settled in France and was married there in 1928. His firstborn (and only son) was Jacques, who was born on

---

[1]Perhaps it is worth noting, on the way by, that Tom started several files on Vatican II, trying to understand the changes that were, and were not, taking place. He has left numerous pages of notes on the documents as he read them.

12 September 1929—which, of course, gave Jacques a grounding in French.[2] This is not the place to retell Jacques's life. It is enough to say that he was profoundly influenced at Wheaton College by Dr. Kenneth S. Kantzer and was challenged to serve in Québec by Ernie Keefe: we have returned to the "jailbirds" once again.

Jacques and his American wife Loretta moved to Québec in June 1963, several months before Tom Carson left Drummondville for Hull. Initially Jacques spent the summer in Asbestos-Danville, giving Ernie and Betty Keefe a much-needed break. When the Keefes returned, Jacques determined that in due course he would plant a work in nearby Victoriaville, which, despite the name, was virtually 100 percent French-speaking. Before making the move to Victoriaville, however, he and Loretta decided that for her sake it would be wiser to spend a year in Sherbrooke, a city of about seventy thousand, where she could work on her French at Institut Biblique Béthel (briefly mentioned in chapter 5 of this book). Sherbrooke could boast three small francophone evangelical churches, none of them at this point particularly effective in outreach. While Loretta studied French, Jacques would assume, for one year, the pastoral leadership of one of these, a small, French-speaking Baptist church.

That one year stretched to eleven. Jacques was, and is, a Type-A personality. From the beginning he was hammering away to open up new evangelistic opportunities. By the end of the first year, he and a team of five others from his little church were visiting door-to-door every Monday night. Then he distributed fifteen hundred pieces of literature inviting people to enroll in a correspondence course on the Bible. He started a small Christian bookstore; he invited students from Bible colleges to spend part of the summer in Sherbrooke, even if they did not know the language, distributing free literature. By this means he blanketed half the city. He thought the annual Sherbrooke Fair might be an appropriate venue, booked a booth, and in one week distributed one thousand books. During this

---

[2]The account of his life and ministry is nicely summarized in the brief biography by Douglas Porter, *The Son of a Wandering Armenian Orphan: A Biography of Jacques Alexanian, Missionary-Pastor in Québec* (Montréal: Éditions SEMBEQ, 2006). The work was simultaneously published in French.

period he still kept his eye on Victoriaville, a city of fifty thousand with no evangelical congregation of any kind. But still he stayed in Sherbrooke, by his own admission somewhat discouraged by the slow growth despite the aggressive effort. In the decade of the seventies, evangelical work in French Canada exploded. From about forty evangelical churches, the work grew to just under five hundred churches and preaching points before settling down to just over four hundred. The turning points were slow but significant. A popular French-Canadian musician, Armand Desrochers, was soundly converted under Jacques's ministry and began to write gospel songs. His first post-conversion album came out in 1969 and opened up a platform. Armand's wife Carmen trusted Christ in 1971. Her baptism was attended by 159 people. At the Sherbrooke Fair in 1972, Jacques secured the films from the "Sermons de la Science" ("Sermons from Science") pavilion at the 1967 World Fair in Montréal. Eight thousand saw them before the Sherbrooke Fair was over. Perhaps more significant yet was the conversion of Claude Laverdière and his wife Suzanne in the summer of 1970. Laverdière was promptly fired from his teaching job. Jacques kept encouraging him with the truth that God had a plan for his life. One of Jacques's efforts in outreach had begun to see a handful of conversions among the six thousand CEGEP and university students in Sherbrooke. In due course, Claude Laverdière became the first full-time campus worker for the French churches of the Fellowship. And in the providence of God, similar outreach onto other CEGEP campuses was bearing fruit in many places around the Province.

One of the challenges that was emerging was how to train these young men—and the overwhelming majority of converts on the campuses were men—quickly enough to meet the needs of the expanding churches. Sending them outside the Province was expensive. Worse, it took them away from their base and from Québec's needs. For many students such an exercise also involved the hurdle of having to learn reasonably fluent English. By January 1974 the decision had been made by Québec French-speaking pastors to begin a training college with no campus, a modified church-based system. Regional churches would be designated, and all courses would be modular. Some TEE

(Theological Education by Extension) courses first developed in Spanish were translated into French, until the Canadians developed more of their own courses. The handful of French-speaking evangelical scholars in North America were invited to fly in for a week to teach modular courses (Roger Nicole was one of the first of these); where no French-speaker was available, English-language professors were brought in from English Canada and from the U.S., and interpreters were assigned. Within eight months, sixty students had signed up for the program. When they were not actually taking courses, they were expected to serve in local churches where they were passing on what they had learned. Thus SEMBEQ (=Séminaire Baptiste Évangélique du Québec) was born.

By 1974 Jacques had been in Sherbrooke for eleven years. The region had grown to two hundred thousand, but the church was well-established and could be led by one of the emerging French-Canadian pastors. It was at that juncture that the Montclair church was without a pastor, and Tom was again serving as interim while holding down his Civil Service job. The leaders asked Tom whom they should consider inviting as the next pastor. Tom's reply was simple: "Go after the best man you can find." It was already clear to most observers that that man was Jacques Alexanian. That perception was confirmed when the General Secretary of the French Association said the same thing. Humanly speaking, the folk at Montclair thought this was a fairly ridiculous invitation to send out: Why should Jacques, currently pastor of the largest and most vibrant church in the Association, accept the challenge of this small, bilingual, struggling church?

But the Lord's timing was in it, and Jacques came in 1974. By the middle of the year, he and his wife and family of six had settled in Hull. He came with the articulated strategy of focusing his own energy entirely on the French side of the work. By August he was already gently insisting that two separate sets of financial books be kept, one of the obvious first steps toward disentangling the congregations. The Fellowship office was asked to look into the possibility of sending someone entirely for the English side. Jacques said such a person would be welcomed with open arms, but that the congregations must be separated or the French side would never grow. Tom was asked to preach pretty regularly on the English side until someone could be appointed. For very good reasons, the proposed independent English work never got off the ground. But the English believers were not abandoned: they could easily drive across the river to attend one of the many English-language churches in Ottawa. By the autumn of 1974, Jacques was getting into his stride and was talking about opening up a booth at the Hull Fair the next summer, bringing up some workers from Sherbrooke, and tackling evangelism in the local CEGEP. By 1977 Jacques knew that his priority must be to train a new generation of leaders. So he started, first in Hull and then throughout the Province, "serviteurs en formation" ("Servants-in-Training")— young men committing themselves to two years of mentoring, usually while taking SEMBEQ courses, with no guarantee of salary. Three rose to the challenge in the Fall of 1977; within less than a decade it was one of the most vital programs in all of Québec.

Within a little over a year of Jacques's coming, the now entirely French-speaking Montclair church was financially independent. Before Jacques left in 1984, four more churches had been planted in the area. The largest was in Gatineau, perhaps a dozen miles away. When it came time to put up a building, Jacques organized the laying of the foundations and then brought in seventy volunteers from Ontario and close to that number again from around Québec, and within forty-eight hours the basic structure of a church building that would seat four hundred was standing. The Gatineau church had drawn off many of the most promising of the Montclair members, but both churches were viable and growing. The Sunday after services first began in Gatineau, there were still ninety-one in the Montclair congregation. While Jacques maintained genial supervision of all five of these churches, increasingly he devoted his own energies to the Gatineau work. Tom, now retired from the Civil Service, provided the leadership and preaching needed at the Montclair church, all in French. In this he was assisted by a young man called André Constant, one of those initial "servants-in-training."

The pace of growth was staggering, and Tom's reactions to these changes initially were complex. But before we take them up and trace some more of his thoughts in his journals, I want to bear my own witness to those remarkable years.

First, I have focused on Jacques not only because he was one of the most fruitful leaders during that remarkable period, but also because he was the next pastor of the Montclair church where Tom and Marg were still serving. But many around Québec were seeing far more growth than anyone had seen in half a century. After the fact, we can poke around and try to understand some of the social dynamics that God used to usher in these changes, but the fact of the matter is that this was a singular movement of God. I finished my PhD in the autumn of 1975 and took up a post in Vancouver on Canada's west coast. Because of my facility in French, it was not long before I was flying back and forth across the country to make minor contributions in *"la belle province"* ("the beautiful province," as Québec was known). In the summer of 1976, I spent a week or ten days teaching a modular course in Sherbrooke. On Wednesday night I was asked to speak at the prayer meeting and Bible study of the church that Jacques had left two years earlier. I asked the pastor how long I had to speak. He replied, "These people are hungry for the Word. I never take less than an hour; as a visitor, you should take more, of course."

I arrived at 7:30. About eighty-five people were present. There was half an hour of reverent singing, some of it freshly written hymns and songs. Shortly after 8:00 I began to preach. I finished just before 9:30. The pastor said this was a wonderful opportunity to ask any question they wanted about what the Bible said. I answered questions until 10:00 P.M. Then prayer requests were solicited, and almost all of them had to do with the conversion of people or the spiritual growth of people to whom these believers were bearing witness. We got down on our knees to pray about 10:30 P.M. I was the first to leave, sometime between 12:30 and 1:00 A.M., as I still had some preparation to do for my class at 8:00 A.M. the next morning. The pastor assured me that this was a fairly normal Wednesday evening.

This degree of intensity was not replicated everywhere around the Province, but in some measure or other it was not rare in the years leading up to about 1980.

Second, what I was discovering when I returned to Québec, whether to Montréal or to Hull or elsewhere, was a new generation of converts who were full of life, vitality, zeal, intelligence, and deep experiences of grace. These were potential leaders, potential pastors, gifted personal evangelists, graduate students. The future lay here. It was simply exhilarating. Most of today's pastors and leaders in the church in French Canada emerged from that extraordinary harvest of young converts.

In the first half of 1974, these changes had not yet come to Hull. Tom, still not remunerated for the long hours he was putting in as interim pastor while still working for the Civil Service, would from time to time be given some kind of thank offering. For instance, on Sunday, 26 May 1974, he records, "Gift for Marg and me for $800 to visit Don in England." That would be used the next year when the Don in question married an English lass called Joy.

Wednesday, June 19, 1974

Meditation: Gen. 29:10: ". . . when Jacob saw Rachel . . . (he) went near, and rolled the stone from the well's mouth, and watered the flock. . . . (19) And Jacob served seven years for Rachel; and they seemed unto him but a few days for the love he had to her." O Lord, I am sixty-two years old; but help me to love my wife the way Jacob loved Rachel.

* Saturday, Dec. 28, 1974

On my knees. "If knowing God is through reading the Bible, then the way to come from darkness to light, from gloom to gladness, is to drop everything to know that book and to follow it. 'Oh that I knew where I might find him,' said Job." Such are the words of one who apparently was finding no relief. Whether he found it or not, I do not know. Perhaps I shall find the rest of his story elsewhere, later on. It would be a most interesting revelation.

Although Tom had publicly supported the coming of Jacques

Alexanian, Jacques's arrival prompted another brief round of introspection and discouragement for Tom. Jacques was competent,
full of ideas, effective in getting things done. He already enjoyed
a track record of success. And initially Tom was being asked to
help the English side in Hull in its transition away from the French
work. For a short while Tom kept away from the French services.
Marg, though, insisted on going and a few times went by herself. Of
course, Tom was soon there with her, and Jacques Alexanian soon
found a multitude of ways to tap into Tom's biblical knowledge and
pastoral experience.

Within a short space of time, the English folk had moved on,
and Tom involved himself exclusively with the French side. Three or
four years later he retired from the Civil Service. Retirement freed
up his time to return to pastoral ministry at the very moment that
the multiplication of congregations under Jacques's ministry meant
there was much more to do.

The difference this time was that Jacques was responsible
for all the organizing and planning. Without demanding more
than Tom's strength could provide, Jacques provided structure,
set goals, and compiled lists of people to visit and lists of young
people to train in doctrine and life or to prepare for marriage.
The brute fact is that Tom functioned better as a number-two
pastor than the senior man. Freed from these sorts of responsibilities, Tom began to flourish again, doing the things he did
best: personal work with young Christians, encouraging those
who needed it, the gift of hospitality and prayer with folk, and
steady, workmanlike preaching that always aimed to be faithful
with the text. He also began a choir. There is no hint in the journal entries that Tom was ever jealous of Jacques. There is always
the most profound gratitude for his gifts, along with increasing
self-awareness that he himself was learning to flourish again
under the younger man's leadership.

It helped, of course, that this was taking place while the
wind of the Spirit was still blowing across French Canada. If
one reads Tom's journal right through for the year 1981—now
almost entirely in French—one is struck by the remarkable

change in tone from the journals written in the bleakest years before Tom's departure from Drummondville. There is only one entry, in the course of the entire year, in which a sense of failure and defeat surfaces. This takes place after Tom and Marg had driven to a conference in Sherbrooke and stopped for a day in Drummondville. There he had made contact, rather fruitlessly and frustratingly, with some of his most difficult and intransigent sheep from past years. This prompts painful reflections on his many failures. Yet there is some irony in this, irony Tom does not even begin to see. How many pastors would return to a former site of ministry and try to contact all of the most difficult people? Would not most contact instead all the bright spots, prayerful supporters, and grateful converts? As I read the entry, even I could call many of the latter to mind and name them. Perennially insecure, Tom did not even glimpse that his choice of whom to visit on that trip through Drummondville served as dramatic witness to the pastoral heart God had given him.

With all the children married and gone from the home, Tom takes Marg out more now, sometimes on his visitation calls. Tom always reserves time to make contact with his children and grandchildren. He notes, for instance, the birth of Cherith, the youngest of Joyce's four daughters, on 11 August.

Many entries summarize the outlines of sermons he is working on or has recently delivered. For instance:

Sunday, Jan. 11, 1984
```
I preached at the Hull church, 1 Cor. 9:19-27: I.
Paul had a goal: to win as many as possible. II. Paul
had an empathetic heart: to become the slave of all
so as by all means to win some. This required deep
understanding of the Christian's place in redemptive
history, with respect to the law. III. Paul had re-
solve: I run, not as uncertainly; I fight, not as one
beating the air.
```

When he lists the people he is visiting, Tom now attaches to each entry the purpose of the visit or what was achieved (details he rarely included in his earlier journals). This sort of entry abounds:

Wednesday, Jan. 28, 1981

I worked hard in my study from 2:30 to 5:45 P.M. This
evening I went to Vanier with Steve, in order to listen to the testimony of some who want to be baptized:
[there follows a list of five names]. The candidates
seem to be genuinely saved.
   A good day.

Tom's pastoral heart is as strong as ever:

Sunday, Feb. 22, 1981

I preached at Hull: 1 K. 18:41–46. . . . J.-G. and
L.B. came for the first time, with M. and R. I weep
for them, caught as they are under the burden of
their sin. O God, may I truly learn that only your
solutions to problems offer real peace and joy.

Tom still sometimes makes lists of things to do and people for
whom to pray, but he seems to be getting them done. A lot of time
is spent not only with those who are just beginning to walk the
Christian way, but with those who are heading toward vocational
ministry. Some of this springs out of a lengthy weekly meeting that
Jacques Alexanian started called "La Pastorale"—essentially an
informal meeting of Jacques and Tom with young pastors, servants-
in-training, and the like. These meetings were slated for Monday
mornings and often went as late as 1:00 or 1:30. They were held at
the home of the Alexanians until 1984. When the Alexanians left to
take up the leadership of SEMBEQ, "La Pastorale" moved to the
Carson home, Marg providing coffee and cookies. These meetings
worked through theological and pastoral issues in considerable
detail, with open Bibles, cool heads, and warm hearts. There was
always an extended time of prayer, not only for each other but especially for the people to whom they were ministering. Tom enjoyed
these meetings immensely, for they played to his strengths (few
knew their Bibles better than he, and his wide reading and advancing years gave him a great deal of pastoral insight). The "Pastorale"
stamped many Québec leaders for the next two decades.
   One entry evokes a wry smile, another hushed praise. The for-

mer is dated Thursday, 19 February 1981. Mum had been taking college courses to improve her French, not least because now there was no English congregation. Tom writes, "I made a small suggestion about her French. There was an explosion. I don't want to write this up." Whether there was too much sensitivity on Mum's part or an unwise deployment of Dad's perfectionism, I shall leave the reader to guess. It was very rare to see Dad and Mum at odds with each other, and even this occasion we know about only because of the journal. As for the entry that evokes hushed praise, on Sunday, 5 July, ten adults were baptized in an open-air service at Lac Beauchamp. For those who remember the early years of ministry in Québec, it is almost impossible to read the lines without fighting back tears of gratitude.

These were happy, fruitful times. Even for a glass-half-empty sort of pastor, 1981 was a great year.

Despite continued blessings, the next year would trigger another sort of declension.

CHAPTER NINE

MARG'S ALZHEIMER YEARS

$\mathcal{L}$ ate in 1982 Marg was mugged. She was walking with another senior citizen in her own quiet neighborhood when someone grabbed her handbag and ran. Instinctively Marg hung on and so fell and dashed her head against the edge of the sidewalk. The only thing she could later remember of the incident was how nice the ambulance attendants were to her.

Within a few weeks those closest to her noticed some changes in her personality. At first they were slight. For several years no one suspected Alzheimer's: this was surely some undiagnosed senile dementia, perhaps triggered by the bang on her head. Initially Tom's response was to encourage Marg to do as many of the things she'd always done as she could, even though the quality of her conversation was gently deteriorating. Spoken French had been a challenge to her all her life, but if she concentrated she could get by. Now what grasp of French she had began to go. From time to time she'd ask if they could drive into Ottawa to go to an English-language service as she was getting nothing out of the French services except the singing (she could read the words and understand).

In 1984 Jacques Alexanian completed ten years in Hull and the surrounding region (often referred to, in French, as "l'Outaouais"). He and his family left for Montréal, where SEMBEQ, which he had helped start, had obtained its own building and needed a strong director if it were to take the next steps forward. In due course Tom's "servant-in-training" André Constant became the pastor of the Montclair church and was joined by his brother Pierre. The "Pastorale" moved to Tom's home. Tom still took on a fair bit of preaching in Montclair and sometimes in surrounding churches, but gradually this was reduced as able young men were beginning to pull their weight. He was brought in for a great deal of pastoral counseling. Perhaps still more strategically, he was pulled into the SEMBEQ orb to translate volume after volume of TEE (Theological Education by Extension) course material from English into French. The following snippets from his journals from 1982 to 1985 give some flavor of these changes.

*Monday, Mar. 29, 1982

I had lunch with C.P. on an extraordinarily serious matter. May God help me to get to the bottom of this business.

La Pastorale: 4 hours; Church Board: three and a half hours; admin for the coming J-BEQ team [groups of students who visited churches and offered help in the summer months], 1 hour; office work in my study, 2 hours. [Ten and a half hours, and that wasn't counting the lunch with C.P.—a not atypical day for this man who was about to turn seventy-one.]

*Thursday, Apr. 1, 1982

Marg and I went to the Orchestra [at the National Arts Centre]. I found the first part magnificent, but after the intermission it sounded to me like dissonant rock and roll without the beat. I shall not get used to Stravinsky.

Sunday, May 2, 1982

Don at Jarvis St. Baptist Church. [That is the full entry. There is no comment on what Dad thought of this turn of the wheel.]

At this period Joy and I were living in Chicago. We tried to get back to Hull once or twice a year, and about this time Dad and Mum would drive down about once every two years. Joy and I were in Hull on Sunday, 27 June, when I preached in French. Dad comments equally on the content of the sermon (he approved!) and the state of my French (again, he approved!), though I do not recall that he said anything to me at the time. In fact, after he was gone I found he had carefully gone through most of the books I had written, often with little ticks or marginal notes or question marks, neatly written in pencil. It was very rare for him to take up such matters with me. Partly, I'm sure, he was always simply a private man; partly, I may have been more of a threat to him than he was to me. One entry has always amused me. Not too long before his death, *Christianity Today* published a long article jettisoning or at least marginalizing penal substitutionary atonement, insisting that the "theory" was based on the Roman judicial system and that other "models" are better supported in the Bible. Three or four others were asked to comment on the article, and I was one of them. In the brief space allotted me, I argued, first, that what the New Testament says about the atonement is not particularly dependent on Roman jurisprudence but is grounded in the Old Testament: it thus comes with divine sanction and the richness of Old Testament teaching on the sacrificial system; and second, I argued that penal substitution is the integrating understanding of the atonement in the Bible that makes sense of all the other things that the Bible says about the death of Christ. Dad scribbled in the margin, "No sign of liberalism here." Perhaps my long years in the university world worried him. He had, after all, been brought up in the heyday of T. T. Shields.

Dad records all his phone calls, letters, and visits with his children and grandchildren, including the following:

Friday, July 30, 1982

```
The important news today is that while I was visit-
ing Marg at Mrs. Steele's [Mum was suffering severely
from diverticulitis, and Mrs. Steele provided the
hour-by-hour care she needed], Don phoned about 2:00
P.M. to say that Joy has had a little girl—Tiffany
Anne—by Caesarean section. . . . The baby weighed
just over seven pounds.
```

* *Saturday, July 31, 1982*

Returned home [from visiting Marg, plus several others in the church] and spent three hours in sermon
preparation for Valleyfield. Left for Valleyfield at
7:20 P.M., arrived at the home of the D. family at
9:15 P.M., and got to my bedroom at 10:15 P.M. Worked
on the sermons until midnight.

* *Tuesday, Nov. 16, 1982*

Up at 6:20 A.M. [Lists prayer time, forty minutes of
memory work in Mark's Gospel, twenty minutes of exercise, prayer time.] Picked up *The Master and His
Disciple* [French version] at L.'s. Stopped at the
pharmacy. Home at 9:15 A.M. Worked on office material, phone calls [Tom lists the names], journal.
Worked on sermons [for about five hours, apart from
lunch]. Went to Aylmer re the forthcoming marriage of
S.H. and L.T. . . . This evening I worked on material
for the chorale and went to get photocopies made of
the next music. . . . Spent an hour at the library,
and one and a half hours in office work. Also today
I brought my wife to the hospital for another scan,
and on the same trip we stopped to visit Mrs. A. in
the hospital. I also dropped off *The Master and His
Disciple* at the home of R.R.

   Must remember to send letter to J., A. and D.L.

* *Saturday, Jan. 1, 1983*

Don, Joy, and Tiffany were still here. Obviously we
spent a lot of time talking together. They left at
7:40 P.M. [When our children were young, we'd leave
about that time of the evening and drive twelve
straight hours while they largely slept, then had
breakfast, and had only about five more hours to go
on this seventeen-hour haul to cover the eight hundred miles between Ottawa and Chicago. On this trip
we noticed how much Mum was slowing up.]

* *Tuesday, Mar. 1, 1983*

In my reading and meditation and prayer, I noted:
(1) Enoch "walked" with God. He did not ask God to
change direction. (2) Rom 8:28—"And we know that all
things work together etc.": these words "we know"
do not come together very often. (3) Consider Mark

5: the demons "besought" him, and he granted their
request; the people of the city "besought" to leave
[AV, "began to pray him"], and he acceded to their
request; the man formerly possessed "besought" him
[AV, "prayed him"] that he might accompany him, but
Jesus did not permit him so to do. [It is the same
verb in Greek as in the French version Tom is using.] A lesson: nothing is more important than the
will of the Master. [Tom was reflecting on how often
Christ's will is expressed in negation, but our duty
is to walk with him still, knowing that Romans 8:28
still holds true.]

On 23 March Tom faithfully records the birth of Jim's last
child, Rachel. On Sunday, 27 November 1983, Tom summarizes
and comments approvingly on the sermon of André Constant
in the morning and the sermon of his brother Pierre in the evening—the former on John 2:12–16, the latter beginning a series
on Ecclesiastes 1:1–11.

Sunday, Jan. 1, 1984

Service at 11:00 A.M. Then Marg and I ate at the Swiss
Chalet. [Meals were becoming slower for Mum, and Dad
had not yet taken over all food preparation, as he
eventually did.] Home about 3:00 P.M. I did not waste
any time, esp. after the sermon by André on redeeming
the time. In the evening Marg spoke of wanting to go
to an English church, but everything moved so slowly
we did not make it. She slept a long time. We read a
chapter of James and a chapter of [Packer's] *Knowing
God*. A pleasant evening.

Monday, Jan. 16, 1984

Marg brought up the subject of the chorale. She said
she felt too old now to participate, especially because of her increasing difficulties in French, and
(perhaps) therefore not feeling at ease with the
members. She can't participate because she doesn't
really know what's going on. [Thereafter Tom sometimes comments that he has brought Marg to the chorale practice, but this is simply so she will not
be left alone. She would sit in the pews and quietly
listen.]

Thursday, Feb. 16, 1984
How quickly time passes away.

About this time Tom sometimes appends, at the bottom of each page, how many fruitful hours of work he put in that day. For Monday, 16 April 1984, the note is "eleven hours of work"; the next day, the same; Tuesday, 15 March, nine and a half hours of work. The totals vary from about five to about eleven. On this last-mentioned day, 15 March, he includes in the total two and a half hours on the "Survey"—i.e., translating the "Survey" of systematic theology into French, commenting that he has spent almost ten hours on that volume so far.

Monday, June 25, 1984
Today I gave myself to the SEMBEQ course on the Pentateuch, Vol. 1. I worked hard.

Friday, Nov. 16, 1984
Marg has been getting the supper late these evenings.

During the next three years, Tom preaches a little less frequently but devotes more pages of his journal to his private meditations. He still tackles more than his share of visitation, but increasingly folk come to his study at home for counsel. Of the two, Mum had been the more frequent and faithful letter-writer to their children, though Dad tended to write every few weeks. By now, however, writing is simply beyond Mum. Her letters taper off, and Dad increasingly picks up the slack. In this period a young woman by the name of Sylvie started boarding with them, and sometimes she took over responsibility for meals. By 1987 there are increasing references in Dad's journals to Mum's ailments, and there is a time of enormous joy and gratitude in 1988.

Wednesday, Jan. 28, 1987
Read Matthew 5—8. Note Jesus' answer to "Are there few that be saved?" And especially note how much emphasis there is in Matthew 5—7 on doing God's will.

Monday, Feb. 16, 1987

I still purpose to go on, with this one great assurance, that God is really God, sovereign, in complete
control, and will complete the warp and woof of His
perfect design, always, and in spite of appearances,
I repeat, in full control. Any other consideration
is amusing to Him: He that sitteth in the heavens
shall laugh.

Monday, Mar. 16, 1987

There have been few accomplishments since Friday. I
did keep up my Bible reading and have finished to
Luke 9. This morning I wondered whether I should
write up some of the thoughts that passed through my
mind; they seemed so rich at the time—about one and
a half hours ago. Since then I have had breakfast,
washed, dressed, made the bed, shaved, took Marg's
blood pressure. Here are some thoughts (Luke 7:1—10):
Re the Roman officer whose servant was sick: First
absolute: "I have never found faith like this, not
even in Israel" (v. 9). Second Absolute (Luke 7:1—29
or 35): "I tell you," Jesus added, "John is greater
than any man (person, Gk.) who has ever lived" (v.
28 [At this point Tom is reading and citing the Good
News Bible.]). The rest of the verse gives much food
for thought: "But he who is least in the kingdom of
God is greater than John" (v. 28). That seems to indicate that John was not in the kingdom: how carefully we must define our terms. . . . Cf. Luke 13:28:
"How you will cry and gnash your teeth when you see
Abraham, Isaac, and Jacob and all the prophets in the
kingdom of God. . . ."
    This further thought: John, in prison, asked Jesus
through his disciples if Jesus was the expected one.
Jesus' answer, in part, is to direct attention to his
deliverance of all kinds of other sufferers—but he
leaves John languishing in prison, and sends him this
challenge: "How happy are those who have no doubts
about me!" (Luke 7:23). What about the chorus "What
he's done for others, He'll do for you"?

Friday, Mar. 20, 1987

I washed the clothes yesterday. It took me longer
than necessary, and I finished about 1:30 this A.M.

Marg is forgetful. I mentioned that Sylvie had ten pairs of socks in the wash, and she said that she should put them in the wash more often, as she (Marg) washes every week. For some time it has been every three or four weeks, and I simply take over. I must take this over consistently.

Thursday, Mar. 26, 1987

I have had some good times with the Word, but have not written down anything particular. Marg has been more or less ailing all week. So I have prepared quite a number of meals. Sylvie also prepared the supper on Tuesday: very tasty. . . . I managed, with a word here and there from Marg, an excellent pot roast. We also had the meeting of the Conseil [Church Council] here on Monday evening—till 11:00 P.M.

Monday, Apr. 6, 1987

I still work slowly. In the period from last entry I missed an excellent opportunity to witness to my barber. Guy L. was at Montclair yesterday: excellent message and engaged in soul-winning. Today I have prayed and read. I seem to be ahead in my reading.

On Monday, 13 April, Tom reports that the doctors now think Marg is suffering from Alzheimer's.

One week later he simply recites a hymn without further comment:

Monday, Apr. 20, 1987

Holy Ghost, with light divine,
Shine upon this heart of mine;
Chase the shades of night away,
Turn my darkness into day.
Holy Ghost, with power divine,
Cleanse this guilty heart of mine.
Long hath sin without control
Held dominion o'er my soul.
Holy Ghost, with joy divine,
Cheer this saddened heart of mine;
Bid my many woes depart,
Heal my wounded, bleeding heart.
Holy Spirit, all divine,

      Dwell within this heart of mine.
      Cast down every idol-throne,
      Reign supreme—and reign alone!

On 20 May 1987 Tom took two hours to write to his grand-daughter Tiffany, about to turn five. Two days later he comments, "Marg now puts thing in various places. So, though I was well occupied before dinner it was in doing things around the stove, helping with dishes, putting pots and pans etc. where I could locate them." From about that point on, Tom simply takes over virtually all household responsibilities. This stage in Mum's degenerating condition became clear to us the next time we were in Hull for a visit. If she helped with the dishes, you could never be sure where she would put anything. At the meal table, she might suddenly dump some marmalade in her tea or spoon sugar onto her potatoes. If anyone gently tried to suggest an alternative, Mum would snap back, "I've been doing this all my life." One of the more helpful resources we read at the time was the book by Nancy L. Mace and Peter V. Rabins, *The 36-Hour Day: A Family Guide to Caring for People with Alzheimer Disease, Other Dementias, and Memory Loss in Later Life.* It laid out very clearly what could be expected at each stage and how best to respond. Many Alzheimer's patients become severely bad-tempered and crotchety. Mum never sank too far into that particular hole, but I am persuaded that this was in no small part because Dad was infinitely patient and kind.

At this period Tom is still working but adding something else into the mix. Increasingly he was being called on to serve as pianist at Montclair. This he takes seriously: many entries read "Piano, 1 hour." He set himself to disciplined practice. On Saturday, 8 July 1987, he mentions this, plus three hours of translation, and then looks back on the previous days and adds, "Yesterday I washed the kitchen floor. Thursday evening I made salad for supper. Yesterday, Marg, Sylvie, and I took a little walk. I read thirty pages in Don's book, *Hermeneutics, Authority and Canon.* It is not an easy book, but in places it is very moving." In October he and Mum traveled to Montréal to see Jim and Lois. Mum stayed

there while Dad went on to an ordination council. His notes show
where he is displeased with the candidate's responses—in this case
his lack of clarity regarding heaven, hell, the general resurrection,
and the intermediate state.

By the next Spring, one entry (7 May 1988) is simply an
extended meditation on 2 Kings 4:1–6:23, and another, after mentioning his early-morning prayer, lists jobs he is doing around the
house, at seventy-six years of age: washing windows, cutting the
grass, ironing clothes, writing letters, and several other things. Right
after he mentions washing windows, he interjects, "And what can
wash away my stain? Nothing but the blood of Jesus." Then he
adds:

> I must really get a hold of Marg's needs. Love her.
> Here I must interject. Oh, I have so much to learn
> about really loving my wife. [I cannot follow the
> path of] R.S. [whom he has been counseling] who in-
> sists it is impossible for him to continue to love
> his wife: there is nothing between them. It's over.
> The thought comes to mind: Does God ever ask His
> children to do that which is impossible for them?
> Then if He asks me—no, tells me—to love my wife,
> then, if I am really "saved," really a child of God,
> I can, with all the resources of what it means to be
> saved. Or if He tells me, as a wife, to submit myself
> to my own husband, then I can—or I am not a Chris-
> tian. And this goes—God help me—for everything He has
> outlined for His children.

And the time of enormous joy? It is best told from Dad's perspective:

Tuesday, June 14, 1988

> Many things have happened since my last entry. . . .
> The major event was the surprise of the fiftieth
> wedding anniversary. Joyce, Den, Sondra and Cherith
> arrived Wednesday, June 8 about 6:00 P.M. Don, Joy,
> Tiffany and Nicholas arrived Friday, June 10, at
> 1:20 P.M. The family brought us to Anderson's res-
> taurant on the island [in the Ottawa River]. We had
> a lovely time at this fairly expensive restaurant.

```
Then they said we were going out the next evening,
but it wouldn't be anything like that, leaving us
the impression it would be on a more modest scale.
We dressed for this surprise, too. Where did they
bring us? To the Gatineau Church where more than two
hundred guests were waiting for us [for a catered
meal], including [a long list of relatives, some of
them unconverted, and close friends]. There was a
presentation of a beautiful sound system and a cheque
for $607.
```

The evening was full of testimony to the grace of God mediated through the lives of Tom and Marg Carson. Mum sat there and smiled sweetly, but at this point she would have understood little of it, even though many parts of the evening were translated because of the presence of anglophone guests. The barrier was no longer linguistic but brain degeneration. And what little she did understand she would not long remember. Dad was frankly bushwhacked by the whole thing. Not for a moment had he anticipated this. In some ways he was replicating the stance of the apostle Paul. Most people go through life afraid that people will not think enough of them; Paul went through life afraid that people would think too much of him (2 Cor. 12:5–6).

There was another way in which Tom's outlook mirrored that of the apostle. When Paul arrived in Athens (Acts 17:16), the Parthenon had been standing for five hundred years, but Paul does not comment on the architecture: Luke tells us the apostle was distressed because of the idolatry. Tom's reflections on his reading—he loved good biographies—betray his fundamental allegiance to moral and spiritual categories of assessment. The entry for a Wednesday in July 1988 reads:

```
I cut the grass this afternoon. I read the sad his-
tory of the life of W.G. [one of the greatest hockey
players the game has ever produced] and his fiancée
who for many years had their own live-in "friends."
A remarkable young man. What does their heart say
when they think of eternity? May God bless their
marriage!
```

> I left supper to Marg. She can't do much, but she
> managed macaroni and cheese. Went to prayer meeting.
> Long discussion afterward with J.-P.M. on the old
> nature.

* *Sunday, Sept. 26, 1988*

> Despite my inconsistencies and the failures that are
> unworthy of a Christian, God in His grace sustained
> me so that I was able to preach at Calvary Baptist
> Church with a certain assurance of His presence, es-
> pecially in the morning. May I always remember God's
> faithfulness!

Inevitably, the relationship between Dad and Mum was changing. They were always pretty careful not to let their kids witness
their disagreements. But when they were a young couple and still
working things out, both, of course, had lessons to learn. My sister
Joyce reports one of these early clashes, told to her only when she
herself had become an adult. Joyce writes:

> I always admired [Mum's] perspective. On one occasion she men-
> tioned something Dad had said to her (can't now recall what it
> was). When I asked how she responded, she sniffed and said that a
> comment like that didn't merit a response, so she gave him none. On
> another occasion she was visiting her doctor, and he was concerned
> about her rising blood pressure. Apparently he asked her how she
> responded when she and Dad had a disagreement. She informed
> him that whenever they did, Dad had his say, then disappeared to
> his office in the basement. Her physician told her that he felt that
> part of her blood pressure problem was because although he knew
> her to be a woman with strong opinions, she was not given the
> opportunity to express them. His counsel was that the next time she
> and Dad disagreed, she was to march right down the stairs, enter
> his office, and have her say. Since Mom always took the advice of
> doctors seriously, she did what he said. Dad was so taken aback
> that he didn't know how to respond. She felt that this incident
> contributed considerably to better communication between them
> in subsequent years.

I have already mentioned that neither parent would permit any of the children to be rude or disrespectful to the other
parent, and Dad was particularly careful to protect Mum in

this respect. Dad often said there was nowhere he'd rather be than at home—and, of course, it was Mum who made it *home*. Sometimes when one parent is gifted athletically, it is easy to poke fun at the awkward one—ostensibly in humor, but so easily degenerating into something quite hurtful. We cannot remember a single occasion when Dad said anything derogatory about Mum. By and large they pulled together. Certainly they worked out their own respective responsibilities around the house. I've already recounted how Mum had earlier taken over the household finances.

But by 1988 Dad had taken over just about everything. Sometimes this sort of takeover was accompanied by the comment, "You know, I could have done that for your mother years ago. Why didn't I do it for her then?" Quite frankly, some of this self-criticism was unrealistic: both were working hard until the onset of Mum's disease.

As Mum descended lower into the abyss of Alzheimer's, Dad lost a soulmate with whom to converse. When she began to lose her motor skills, Dad would half pull her to her feet and walk backward, drawing her along with his hands, to get her to walk the short distance to the bedroom or bathroom. She would teeter back and forth, yet prove very slow about putting a foot forward with each teeter, and thus a five-second walk became a twenty- or thirty-minute exercise. The tasks multiplied. External ministry just about evaporated: Dad's ministry was looking after Mum. And not once, *not once*, did any of his children hear a single note of self-pity or a muttered "This isn't the woman I married" or any such thing. We cannot recall a single time when he lost patience with her. He sang to her a great deal and found a funny side to almost everything.

Many entries in his journal find Tom reflecting on Scripture he has been reading, but increasingly he is turning over in his mind just how Mum is doing. Almost always he is a bit too optimistic about her abilities: brute reality has to intrude before he comes to terms with the next level of descent.

Wednesday, July 12, 1989

Many things have occurred since my last entry. Marg's memory has deteriorated greatly. Jim and family were here over the weekend, Friday late (10:00 P.M.) to Monday (4:00 P.M.). By Monday evening she had no recollection of their visit. She has also had three "accidents" . . . for which we had prepared. She can scarcely walk. It's strange: she can get up from the bed, the kitchen chair, the couch in the front room, and walk. Yet she likes to feel secure when I am around and reaches for my hands to get up. When she does so, and I start to walk backwards towards wherever we are to go, so as to hold both her hands, she does not take a step forward but leans back. It is difficult. She scarcely eats her meals; she is almost terrified of sitting so low as the toilet seat in the bathroom; she does not do her hair, wash herself, clean her teeth, but is fairly docile when I do these things for her. In conversation, in understanding, she seems clear, but because of the extreme shortness of her memory never seems able to express even a short thought or desire. She seems "inquiète" at what is happening [Dad uses the French word for "worried" or "anxious," literally "unquiet"]. And I feel so helpless to enter into her processes. I could weep endless tears for not having been a better husband when she was so keen and now it is too late, but I want to do everything for her that a good husband will do.

Jim is a great help. Although I had intended to get in touch with the CLSC [Centre Local de Services Communautaires = Local Community Service Centre, i.e., Québec's social services], he was the one who did it first—from Montréal. Things are moving because of that. He even stayed over Monday, a working day, to meet with the CLSC representative, Mme Gabrielle Gagnon.

Both Joyce and I and our respective families lived a long distance away; so a highly disproportionate burden fell on Jim and Lois, then living in greater Montréal, about two hours away by car. They drove up to Hull with increasing frequency. Often Dad would get on the phone with Lois to ask about how to clean something or cook something. Jim took on more projects around Dad's house on weekend excursions up to Hull. Lois took Mum and Dad's mending home with her, bringing it back a week or two later. Any suggestion from the family that Dad needed help with Mum would earn the firmest insistence that he could look after her himself. "She looked after me all my life," he would say; "it's my turn to look after her. And it's a privilege."

But one night Dad couldn't get Mum out of the bath: she had become almost a dead weight. After trying for forty-five minutes, he called emergency services. The upshot was that the social security system in Québec sent in a district nurse two or three times a week to bathe Mum, do her hair, and so forth. But it wasn't too long before one evening Mum fell in the bathroom, and Dad couldn't get her up. The ambulance took her to the long-term care wing at the local Hull hospital, barely a mile from their home. She never came home again.

The decision to keep her in palliative care would not have been taken at this time if Jim had not been present for the assessment. At the hospital a social worker was making an evaluation. When this social worker asked about Mum's abilities in this or that area, Dad would intimate that Mum was not too bad, even pretty good in that area, until Jim chipped in and reminded him of some incident or other, and Dad would concede that, well, yes, Mum might have a severe problem there. The outcome was a slightly grudging acceptance that Mum had to stay in the palliative care unit.

Of course, that modified Dad's schedule again. Every single day to the end of Mum's life, Dad was at the hospital, usually three times a day (morning, afternoon, evening), occasionally only two times. He would slip out for the regular services at Montclair—not at this time preaching (there simply wasn't time for preparation) but regularly playing the piano. At the hospital, as long as she could walk haltingly down the corridor, he walked with her. As often as possible he fed her. When she was bedridden, he talked with her, sang quietly to her, read Scripture to her, brought in pictures of the children and grandchildren, read letters and cards to her. Soon she lost the ability to speak. For the final few weeks there was only a vacant stare until

someone sang an old hymn such as "Blessed Assurance": that would
win a slight squeeze of the hand. So also would some Scripture readings or photos of the grandchildren. Finally, of course, there was no
response. None at all.

His journal entries circle around three poles: his biblical meditations, his assessment of Mum's condition, and various pastoral
concerns—for people with problems kept trying to see him during
this period, and he would visit them or meet with them at his own
home between trips to the hospital.

The last entry for 1989 is the only one I shall preserve here as
he wrote it, in French, before translating it:

Sunday, Dec. 31, 1989

Marg est allée auprès de son Sauveur. Quelle femme de
Dieu a-t-elle été! Je bénis Dieu de me l'avoir don-
née. Et maintenant il l'a reprise. O Dieu, elle me
manque. Conduis-moi.

  Marg went to be with her Savior. What a woman of
God she was! I bless God for having given her to me.
And now He has taken her back. O God, I miss her.
Guide me.

A little more should be told about Mum's homegoing. It was a
Sunday morning, New Year's Eve, just six days shy of Mum's eighty-
first birthday. Dad, as usual, was at Montclair, playing the piano
for the morning service. The hospital saw that Mum was slipping
away but could not get hold of Dad on the phone. They phoned
Jim in Montréal. Owing to a snowstorm, he had not driven to Hull
that morning, and for the same reason he had not been able to get
to church. He phoned the church number in Hull, and Dad was
pulled out of the service. He was thus able to spend the last couple
of hours of Mum's earthly life with her, by her bedside, praying with
her, holding her hand, still quietly singing. She gave a couple of last
gasps, he called out "Marg!" and she was gone.

My family and I were living in England that year. That evening,
New Year's Eve (Cambridge is five hours ahead of Hull), Dad
phoned me with the news. I was supposed to fly out two days later,
on 2 January 1990, to Australia via Singapore to speak at a large

CMS (Church Missionary Society) conference at Katoomba, in the Blue Mountains, just outside Sydney. I phoned them immediately, of course, and told them I could not come and started making arrangements to fly to Canada instead. Before these arrangements could be put into place, Dad phoned back. He and Jim had been talking at length, and they had a suggestion. In many ways, of course, we had all said our good-byes to Mum a long time before: that is the nature of this awful disease. They suggested I fly to Hull for the memorial service, and, if it wouldn't make me too late, then fly on to Australia from there, heading west to get there instead of east. (Dad knew my schedule intimately, of course, for it was incorporated into his prayer life.) I vacillated, then agreed, and phoned the folk in Sydney again. I flew out of Heathrow to Canada early the next morning, spent less than two days in Hull, and arrived in Sydney a few hours before my first address. That series of talks became *A Call to Spiritual Reformation: Priorities from Paul and His Prayers.*

Monday, Jan. 15, 1990

On my knees I am often crushed. David said, "My sin is ever before me." And mine are ever before me. . . . My wife was a magnificent woman: she rested utterly in the absolute assurance that God had fully forgiven all her sins: "What need I fear when thou art near / And thinkest, Lord, of me?" And I found rest in meditating on Psalm 51.

CHAPTER TEN

ENDING WELL: FINAL MINISTRY AND PROMOTION TO GLORY

*T*he letters and cards poured in. Two or three came from Australia, from Christians who had never met Dad. Many offered traditional condolences, but a surprising number, some in English and some in French, said things like this:

Dearest Mr. Carson,

We were very sorry to hear the news. We know that Mrs. Carson lived a full, rich life in the service of Christ and we rejoice that she is in the presence of the One she loved so much. We are happy to know her suffering is finally over. . . . But we also remember you in your grief. We know how much you loved her—so often we were inspired by how highly you always spoke of her. Truly, we have never seen such love and respect in any other marriage, and we hold your sacred bond as an example. . . . You who have comforted so many, may you now find comfort in your affliction from the Father of mercies and God of all comfort. "For just as the sufferings of Christ are ours in abundance, so also our comfort is abundant through Christ."

With much love in Christ,
L.-M. and A.

Tom's journals show that he thought of himself as a poor husband. This is simply not how he was perceived. He had promised

more than fifty years earlier that he would cherish his wife "for better, for worse, for richer, for poorer, in sickness and in health," and
by God's grace he kept his word.

One family sent in the famous words of Pastor Drelincourt
(1595–1669):

> Adieu, my dear relatives, my precious friends! I rise
> to God, I am going to my Father. The struggles are
> over, and I abandon my misery and exchange today the
> earth for the heavens.
>
> By faith, dry the tears from your eyes, banish from
> your hearts all bitter sadness, and if your love for
> me was ever sincere, reflect on my joy and be happy
> for me.
>
> Ah! but my lot is wonderful! It is worthy of envy.
> By death, I pass to the domain of life, and in dying
> lose nothing but mortality.
>
> Follow me, with vows of hope and zeal. If death
> separates us for a limited time, God will unite us
> in eternal glory.
>
> *The S. family.*

In just under three years, Tom would follow Marg into eternity.
How does he spend his last three years on this earth?

Pretty soon he is on the regular teaching and preaching rota-
tion for the Montclair church, sometimes preaching at others in
the Outaouais. His visitation list is extensive. He travels more often
now, invariably to see the family—most often to see Jim and Lois
because of their proximity, but sometimes driving eight or nine
hundred miles to see his other children and their families (both
Joyce and I at that time lived in Illinois). His letters become longer
and chattier, his phone calls the same: almost certainly this is one
of his ways of combating loneliness. His work with "La Pastorale"
continues every week. Glimpses of the man who stands up for principle surface in new ways. In 1991, when he was almost eighty, he
received a ticket for parking his car in a "Disabled" parking space.
It was unthinkable that Dad would do such a thing wittingly. He
went back to the scene with a camera, waited until a van was parked
in the adjacent slot (thereby covering up one of the signs on the

asphalt) since a van had been there when his own car was ticketed, observed the snow that covered the asphalt on his slot, and took photographs, showing that the sign that was supposed to be on the post was absent. Then he went to court, without a lawyer, and argued his own case, complete with weather reports for the day in question, plus his own photographs. Needless to say, he won. For him, it was a matter of principle.

But he was slowing down. The pastors of Montclair, André and Pierre Constant, phoned me several times to ask how best they could help him with the physical work around the house without being rude. When they had approached him to offer this or that service—washing the windows, say, or cutting the grass or shoveling the snow—he would always protest that he was doing all right and wouldn't want to impose on the church this way. Eventually I suggested they simply show up with a team, bright and cheerful, with some such remark as "Mr. Carson, we've come to cut the grass." If they asked permission, he would decline; if they announced why they had come, he himself would feel it rude to refuse them. This worked out pretty well.

For the first six months after Mum's death, Tom's journals hold a lot of regrets and contrition, bordering on the despair he had experienced toward the end of the Drummondville years. Then they begin to change. Some of the old regrets and self-blame still surface from time to time, of course, but even these are soon bathed in gratitude for the grace of God. For instance, on Thursday, 12 December 1991, two years after her death, he writes:

> Ah, Margaret, we will see each other again, and you
> will no longer remember the multitude of my failures
> that stand before me now, the failures for which I am
> deeply culpable, the unfaithfulness of my life as a
> pastor-missionary. . . . "Behold, I make all things
> new." "And I shall see Him face to face / And tell
> the story, saved by grace." He will wipe away every
> tear, and the enormity of my sin, of my sins, he will
> remember no more forever—for the blood of Jesus, the
> precious blood cleanseth even me from my sin. Oh,
> that I might never sin again. And one day I shall

not, for I shall see Him face to face, and I shall
be like Him, for I shall see Him as He is. "I have
but one supreme desire, / That I might be like Jesus". . . . Margaret will see me as one who is holy,
pure, good, lovable.

Many entries in the journal are long and discursive. His notes
on his visits now often include not simply the purpose of a visit
but a fairly detailed summary of what took place, especially if he
learned some story of the grace of God in the person's life. His biblical meditations find him working out exactly what is being said in
passages—not just recording passing observations but more detailed
theological integration.

Two theological subjects that drew his attention repeatedly
all his life surface here too. The first is the relationship between
the Testaments. He was constantly reflecting on Sabbath/Sunday
debates, for instance, not as an end in themselves but as a test case
for how to put his Bible together. The second is his understanding of
Roman Catholicism. For example, on the latter subject we find:

Tuesday, Feb. 25, 1992

I heard a priest being interviewed on a French [radio]
station at the time of the Billy Graham crusade, and
he was asked point-blank why the R. C. authorities
did not come out and denounce it as presenting much
that could be construed as against Roman Catholic
teaching, though not verbally stated. He hemmed and
hawed, but said in effect it was better to leave the
crusade alone. I could have told them why: because
this upright man that is Billy Graham, his personal
life beyond reproach, is the Roman Catholic church's
best ally, since he welcomed them as evangelicals at
his services. Graham is Jehoshaphat with Ahab.

Often now there is a warmth and genial tenderness to the
entries.

Wednesday, May 1, 1992

This morning I was up at 6:30 A.M. and in my study
just before 8:00. I felt the tremendous need to pray,

and did so. God gave me refreshing. Then I read Judges 8:1 to 9:56: the account of Abimelech. The passage 9:1—21 moved me. Abimelech had had all the sons of Gideon killed; one, the youngest, managed to escape. He went and stood on Mount Gerizim—Sichem, where Abimelech lived, is between mounts Gerizim and Ebal—and shouted a parable. The trees wanted to choose a king. They asked, in turn, the olive tree, the fig tree, and the vine to accept the crown. The olive tree said, in effect, "No, I cannot forsake my oil, because of which people honor both God and men." The fig tree said, "No, I cannot give up my fruit, so excellent and sweet, so that I can rule over other trees." And the vine said, "No, I cannot give up my wine, which makes both God and men rejoice, in order to lord it over the trees." [Here Tom acknowledges that the point of the fable is that these fruitful trees then make a serious mistake: they therefore appoint the thornbush to be king. But while he recognizes that is the point, he insists that before we arrive at that point we must see that God did in fact make the trees to exercise different functions. He goes on:] Each of us Christians has something special to give. [He then runs through a variety of aptitudes and gifts, noting, in line with 1 Corinthians 12, that no one has all the gifts.] When I was in Sunday School as a boy at Calvary Baptist Church, there was a saying hanging from one of the walls where everyone could see it: "I am but one, but I am one; I cannot do everything, but I can do something; what I can do, I ought to do; and what I ought to do, God helping me, I will do." "She has done what she could" (see John 12:1—8; Mark 14:3—9).

As he had done in the past, so too in these years he often quotes hymns and other poetry as the must succinct summary of what he is thinking and praying about.

Wednesday, Apr. 6, 1992
My soul is night, my heart is steel,
I cannot think, I cannot feel.
For light and life I must appeal
In simple faith to Jesus.

The discipline of maintaining a working knowledge of the biblical languages over the years now sometimes issues in lengthy quotations of the Greek text. On Friday, 28 August 1992, he begins by citing 1 John 2:1–2 in Greek and then builds his meditation on the text he has just written down.

Scattered through the journals of his last two years of life are lines like these: "Keep me from the sins of old men"—some of which he details: a tendency to gravitate toward watching television, the temptation to look backward instead of forward, sliding toward self-pity, easy resentment of young men. "Develop, as a senior, a prayer ministry: God has given you the time for it." "God had a plan to take Mum home and a plan to leave me here." Within the last year of his life, Dad thanks God that all his children love God more than he does. This was a sensationally inaccurate evaluation, of course, but a man who thinks such things is not likely to be alienated from his children, as so many fathers are. In his journal entry of 21 August 1991, 4:47 A.M., written half in English and half in French, Dad talks about his deepening experience of God during the previous few days, especially his heightened awareness that all of his acceptability before God turns on the gospel of the death and resurrection of Jesus Christ. He writes out, from memory (I have made two or three corrections), the words of a classic hymn:

> Alas, and did my Saviour bleed,
> And did my Sovereign die!
> Would He devote that sacred head
> For such a worm as I!
>
> Well might the sun in darkness hide,
> And shut His glories in,
> When Christ, the mighty Maker, died
> For man the creature's sin.
>
> Here will I hide my blushing face
> When His dear cross appears,
> Dissolve my heart in thankfulness
> And melt mine eyes in tears.

But drops of grief can ne'er repay
The debt of love I owe.
Here, Lord, I give myself away—
'Tis all that I can do.

Help me, dear Saviour, Thee to own
And ever faithful be;
And where Thou sittest on Thy throne,
Dear Lord, remember me.

On Labor Day weekend (or, as it is in Canada, Labour Day weekend) 1992, Jim and Lois and their children took a vacation in a small cabin only a few hours from Hull and invited Dad along. He gladly went, driving there for several hours in the early morning. He spent the day canoeing and chatting and enjoying his family but insisted on driving back home that evening: he was scheduled to play the piano at Montclair for the services the next day. A few days later he preached his last sermon, just over six weeks before he died. Toward the end of September Dad developed a persistent cough, then a fever. He stopped eating. But, of course, he was unlikely to call anyone for help: he wouldn't want to "disturb" them. In God's providence, Joyce phoned from Illinois. Finding him in terrible shape, she promptly called the pastors of the church, who bundled him off to the Emergency Room. He never came home again—not, at least, that home.

My last letter to him was written from England, where we were again living, on 21 September 1992. It reached him just before he went into the hospital: it was on his pile to be answered. His own last missive was posted a couple of days before he went into the hospital. It was sent to Rebekah Carson, one of Jim's children, apologizing because he didn't think he was going to be able to make it to Montréal for her fourteenth birthday on 2 October since he wasn't feeling very well. Dad never missed the birthdays of Jim's children since they were the ones within driving distance.

During those weeks Jim and sometimes Lois went back and forth between Montréal and Hull constantly. On many days during the final three weeks Jim drove to Hull after work (two hours), spent a couple of hours with Dad, then drove home again. Christians from Montclair were diligent in surrounding him with love and care. Eventually it became clear that Dad was unlikely to survive: his lungs kept filling up. Jim kept in contact with Joyce and me, of course. Joyce flew up to Hull. When it became clear just how serious things were, I flew over from England, arriving two days before Dad died. He was still lucid, though weak. There was time to pray, to talk, though at that point he was not saying much.

Throughout those three weeks, Dad faced a great deal of pain, but as far as those observing him could tell, no fear. Typically, no word of complaint fell from his lips. On one occasion the nurses remarked to Jim, "*Mon Dieu, qu'il sait souffrir!*"—"God, he sure knows how to suffer!" Jim passed on the remark and earned Dad's last rebuke: "Don't say that." The pained look on his face might have been because he did not want God's name to be taken in vain, even in a reported utterance, or because he found it hard to accept positive evaluations of his display of Christian graces. Most likely it was both.

One more small tragedy was about to unfold. On Dad's last day, 26 October 1992, Joyce had briefly left owing to other responsibilities and was about to return. For some time Dad had been slipping in and out of consciousness; by that afternoon he was in a coma. That Monday was a critical election day in Québec, and Jim, ever his father's son, knew to put duty first and drove home to Montréal to vote, expecting to return the next day. Besides, I was there to hold vigil. About 11:30 P.M. I checked with the nursing staff, and they thought he was stable. I had crossed too many time zones, so I decided to go to Dad's house, where I was staying, have a shower and get into some clean clothes, snooze (I have always been able to be refreshed from fifteen minutes of sleep), and come back. I drove to Dad's home, less than five minutes away by car, walked in the door, and the phone rang. It was the hospital: "There has been a change." I raced back to the hospital. Dad was gone, and he had died alone.

The building of the Gatineau church was used for the memorial service: it was much bigger than the Montclair building, and it was packed. Charisse, one of Joyce's daughters and the oldest of Dad's grandchildren, sang "Find Us Faithful." "That was Grandpa," she said. At the wake, the quiet testimonials seemed unending. One young woman who was an attaché at one of the African embassies said that not long before, she had been in intensive care for over a month with postpartum complications. She was in a comatose or semi-comatose state, unable to communicate. She said that "Mr. Carson" had come in every day, sat with her, read Scripture to her, and prayed with her. I found no record of these visits in his journal. During Dad's final stay in the hospital, this woman prepared a room in her home for him in the hope that he would be discharged and that she would have the privilege of nursing him back to health. Another couple spoke with both Joyce and me. They had been having severe marriage problems and were on the brink of divorce. For two years "Mr. Carson" visited them every week and took them through a Bible study on what a godly home and marriage look like. With tears in their eyes, they expressed profound thankfulness for his godly investment in their lives. Some of these visits are briefly alluded to in his journals, but one would never guess from the entries what had gone on. Why should such matters be reported? Tom was simply serving as an ordinary pastor.

He was buried beside his wife under a joint tombstone. It was a simple design, with a cross and a sheaf of wheat meant to evoke Jesus' words, "I tell you the truth, unless a kernel of wheat falls to the ground and dies, it remains only a single seed. But if it dies, it produces many seeds" (John 12:24, NIV). The names and dates of Dad and Mum are there, of course. For an inscription, Tom had toyed with using the words of Philippians 1:23: "I desire to depart and be with Christ, which is better by far" (NIV). But, of course, whatever words he chose would have to be in both English and French, and that seemed too much. So the inscription simply reads, "With Christ / Avec Christ."

Tom Carson never rose very far in denominational structures, but hundreds of people in the Outaouais and beyond testify how much he loved them. He never wrote a book, but he loved the Book. He was never wealthy or powerful, but he kept growing as a Christian: yesterday's grace was never enough. He was not a farsighted visionary, but he looked forward to eternity. He was not a gifted administrator, but there is no text that says, "By this shall all men know that you are my disciples, if you are good administrators." His journals have many, many entries bathed in tears of contrition, but his children and grandchildren remember his laughter. Only rarely did he break through his pattern of reserve and speak deeply and intimately with his children, but he modeled Christian virtues to them. He much preferred to avoid controversy than to stir things up, but his own commitments to historic confessionalism were unyielding, and in ethics he was a man of principle. His own ecclesiastical circles were rather small and narrow, but his reading was correspondingly large and expansive. He was not very good at putting people down, except on his prayer lists.

When he died, there were no crowds outside the hospital, no editorial comments in the papers, no announcements on television, no mention in Parliament, no attention paid by the nation. In his hospital room there was no one by his bedside. There was only the quiet hiss of oxygen, vainly venting because he had stopped breathing and would never need it again.

But on the other side all the trumpets sounded. Dad won entrance to the only throne room that matters, not because he was a good man or a great man—he was, after all, a most ordinary pastor—but because he was a forgiven man. And he heard the voice of him whom he longed to hear saying, "Well done, good and faithful servant; enter into the joy of your Lord."

THE LETTER OF 5 MAY 1948

*F*or the historical context in which this letter was sent, see Chapter 4 above.

Box 473,
Drummondville, P.Q,
May 5, 1948

Dear Brethren,

Before answering, in some measure at least, the letter sent out to all our churches on behalf of the Executive Board of our Union, I want to say that the property under option has been secured, and we have placed $10,000 insurance on it, at a cost of $170 for three years. The deal was put through over my signature. As soon as registration is made we shall have the property transferred to the Snowdon Baptist Church till such a time as we are able to assume full responsibility as a Baptist church in this province. To God alone we give glory for His mighty help, and in this great opportunity for reaching French-Canadians we count on Him to multiply His mercies and blessings.

When I read the letter sent out by the Executive Board, I was simply amazed. I give, therefore, my own testimony.

The story of the beginnings in Drummondville are probably well known. Rev. Morley R. Hall, whose recognized gift in the pioneering of new causes had been the main reason for his being asked several years ago to give leadership in such work here, had visited the Eastern Townships looking for a strategic field for missionary work. After much prayer and thought Drummondville was chosen as presenting the greatest opportunity, having already "earnest believers . . . who were weary of the sawdust menu supplied them in modernistic churches . . . glad to come to the new restaurant for a meal." (A statement of Home Mission Policy, adopted as a general statement of policy and passed by the Executive Board, April 6, 1948.) As for the opportunity for French-Canadian evangelization, it is simply tremendous (see Convention Report, 1947, Mr. Hall's and my letters on Drummondville Baptist Building Fund campaign). Mr. Hall assured these people [in Drummondville] that we meant business, and I felt it my ordinary responsibility to do what I could to help.

When, therefore, by the return of Mr. Oatley-Willis to the Seminary, and the illness of Rev. F. Kegel the carrying on of these meetings [in Drummondville] seemed impossible, I undertook to go for the Sunday evening service, following my two French services in Montréal. I had not thought then of moving to Drummondville. At that time I was hoping to have help to purchase a permanent place in Montréal where we might centralize our work there.

At the 1947 Convention, a Committee approached me asking if I would consider moving to Drummondville, suggesting even the possibility of the Board's putting up quarters for meetings and parsonage. I had still not conviction that I should go, and could give no forthright answer within the time limit—the short period of less than twenty-four hours.

During those days the Convention approved the following statement concerning Drummondville, laid down in the Board's report: "The need of a building is most urgent; even this Fall something may have to be done if we are to hold the ground already taken" (p. 10). In harmony with the expressed wish of the messengers of the churches meeting in Convention, and the need of the work in Drummondville, we began looking over locations. The property believed to be the best and most strategically placed was carefully considered, and heartily endorsed by the First Com-

mittee appointed by the Board, by the people themselves, and by me.

The letter sent to the churches by the Board gives
the impression that the property was away from the
people. It states that the second Committee "felt
the property was not as well located as was desir-
able. . . . [In fact it] ought to be said that the
house proposed was about three blocks distant from
the limit of the city of Drummondville and at the
very end of the bus line." The last part of the sentence is not correct. The bus turns at the corner on
which our property is situated—the local Drummondville bus, no extra fare—to go still farther through
this section of St-Simon. As far as the location of
the property is concerned, the letter says nothing
of the fact that St-Simon has already a population of
some 3,000, that a good many new streets have been
cut through, lots surveyed, most of which are bought
up, and that the building forecast for even this year
is "simply stupendous." Our building is in the heart
of that activity. Nor can one readily tell where St-
Simon begins and Drummondville ends.

Furthermore, the property itself is every bit as
reasonable as any other in all Drummondville. I am
certain that the second Committee had nothing better
to suggest, and at the same time even comparable in
the way of location and utility.

It was during this period of investigation I came
to realize some of the possibilities and prospects
open to us in Drummondville. All that brother Hall
had written concerning its strategic value was true,
and I began to feel a drawing towards it. As I stated
in my letter to the churches on Feb. 19th, "Our four
years experience trying to cover the huge area of
greater Montréal has convinced us of the necessity
of concentrating our efforts on a given centre in order to do French work most effectively. In Montréal
every effort to obtain an essential building has
thus far come to nought. But in Drummondville—Greater
Drummondville has a population of some 30,000 [sic;
should read 50,000], 95% of whom are French-Canadian
Roman Catholics—we have a nucleus of [English-speak-
ing] Christians, to whom it has been our privilege to
minister from week to week since last October, sufficiently interested to look after the subsequent mort-

gage payments (amounting the first year to approxi-
mately $900.00), and who are anxious to see the work
go ahead. Montréal will not be left uncultivated. But
where we may concentrate, there we believe we ought
specially to labour." And when I became convinced of
this opportunity as one which must not be lost, as a
field which must and could be thus entered, I gave
myself completely to what I believed was a definite
call from the Lord.

The first Committee, who had carefully considered
the matter, sought help for this undertaking through
the Finance Committee, but the latter did not arrive
at any definite conclusion.

About the second week of January [1948] I was fully
convinced that if this work [in Drummondville] was
to go on we must locate in a place of our own. How
could we expect to evangelize French-Canadian Roman
Catholics using a school kindly and generously placed
at our disposal for our English services, but whose
owner was an English-speaking Roman Catholic? What
freedom of spirit would we have in continuing under
obligation to one of those we believed to be in great
error spiritually and whose powerful Church abomi-
nates our message, especially when it is delivered
in the French language? What possibility would there
be of continuing? Yet that is what the Board in its
letter to the churches suggests: "It was decided to
continue the work in Drummondville as we have done,
using the place of meeting that has been used since
last summer." As a matter of fact the proprietor
asked me three months ago when we expected to be able
to move. Think of my telling her, "It was decided,
etc. etc.!"

Furthermore, what about the believers here? In a
letter to brother Hall dated Mar. 20, 1948, I wrote
concerning them, "We owe them a debt we shall never
be able to repay; for somehow, through the years they
have kept the flame of the Gospel alight in face of
tremendous discouragement, and made such an entrance
as ours into this needy place possible." I refer
you again to the quotation at the beginning of this
letter, that there were already "earnest believers
. . . glad to come. . . ." This quotation, I repeat,
is taken from the general statement of policy passed
April 6, 1948, by the Executive Board itself.

Thus, in procuring a site as the one proposed, we should have a place of our own, with a group of believers, in a great centre with almost unlimited opportunity for French-Canadian evangelization. And that, to my mind, is by far the most effective way in which to approach French work in Québec.

Many such considerations urged me on, and, as our real estate agent had promised to keep the property for us until the end of January, after laying the matter before the Lord and our people, I set out alone, about the middle of January to try to raise the $5,000 required for the cash deposit.

However, just before going I took a very definite stand. Believing that if we should obtain this property the Roman Catholic Church might come down hard upon our real estate friend, and, as a consequence he might be lost to us as far as any possibilities of reaching him for Christ were concerned, I told him exactly who I was, how I had learned my French, and "preached unto him Jesus." Then I asked if he were willing still to do business with us. He said that he was, that his Church permitted him so to do. Events have proved that he was willing. I left his home, at first feeling that I had thus given up our chances of getting that building. But God gave me a text that day: "Them that honour me, I will honour." Let who will charge it to fancy, emotionalism, sentiment. To me, it was the voice of the Lord.

I told brother Armstrong [the pastor of Snowdon Baptist Church in Montréal] of my resolution. Two or three whom I approached for help urged me to get the backing of the Board, but I said that the Finance Committee was unwilling to do anything at the present time.

After having visited several outside points I returned to Montréal and discovered that a meeting of the Finance Committee had been called for Jan. 23rd to deal with the matter of Drummondville. In the minutes of the meeting we find the following:

After a full discussion it was moved . . . and seconded . . . that Messrs. Armstrong, Carson, and Hall be appointed as a Committee to go into further details regarding the Drummondville proposition for the purpose of ascertaining all

the facts relative to this property including
taxes, improvement tax, the dimensions of rooms,
and such information as would assist in making
decision; and furthermore that inquiry be made
if an option could be procured and the amount
of same which would afford sufficient time for
Mr. Carson to canvass the churches of our Union;
and whether in the event of $5,000 being raised
the balance could be carried as a mortgage, and
the same Committee to report back as early as
possible.

It was also requested that Mr. Carson be asked
to meet the Finance Committee in person in order
that he might state his personal convictions regarding his call to the work in Drummondville.

Mr. Armstrong and I obtained the further details
sought. We enquired concerning an option. As I had
been making enquiries and had already obtained time
for nothing, our agent felt he could not keep on doing that. I thought him to be perfectly justified
in his attitude. He had given me until the end of
January—the Finance Committee meeting was called for
Feb. 6th—and he said he did not see his way clear
to give more free time. His man was pressing him to
sell. So, on Jan. 28th, feeling hopeful that there
was some possibility of help, realizing it would give
me more time should the Finance Committee not see
its way clear to do anything, after consulting with
certain of the Drummondville friends, I signed for an
option on the excellent Mercure Boulevard property,
option to expire April 1, 1948. We turned over from
our Drummondville funds the $500 required. We agreed
to buy the property for $13,500, for which the owner
had originally asked $15,000, $5,000 cash, $8,500 in
mortgage agreements.

On Feb. 6th, 1948, the Finance Committee had its
meeting. After a long session at which I was not
present they called me and told me the decision. Here
it is in part:

    . . . it is resolved that the report of the
    Committee be adopted and that an effort be made
    to raise the $5,000 in new money from our Union
    constituency with the understanding that the ma-

jor drive must take place during April and May
. . . and inasmuch as the $5,000 must be paid
before the expiration of the option, it is understood that whatever new money can be procured
before that date shall be used as a gift to the
Drummondville work and the balance to make up
the $5,000 be borrowed by the Board on its own
collateral and that after the 31st of March a
concerted effort be made to raise enough money
to free the Board's collateral by paying off the
loan, and that the whole $5,000 then be a gift
to the Drummondville work.

And that when the property is purchased until
such time as a Regular Baptist Church shall be
recognized and incorporated in Drummondville,
the property should be vested in the Snowdon
Regular Baptist church of Montréal and subject
to the same credal statement as is contained in
their Constitution.

And if, in the happy circumstances of the appeal resulting in more than $5,000 received,
then that amount should be used to reduce the
amount of the Mortgage also as a gift.

It is needless to say that my heart sang. Mr.
Armstrong and I returned home [from Toronto to Mon-
tréal] that night. The very next evening he telephoned me. After we had gone, another meeting of the
Finance Committee had been called. I quote from the
minutes:

. . . After considerable discussion, and in
view of the fact that an earnest effort was to
be put forth among our churches for the establishing a work in Drummondville, _____ and _____
moved the rescinding of their motion of Friday,
February 6th, 1948. This being agreed to, the
following was moved by _____ and seconded by
_____:

Resolved that we authorize the immediate
launching of a building campaign, under the
supervision of the Finance Committee, for Drummondville, to be concluded by May 31st, and
that Mr. Carson be requested to continue his
services in Drummondville as at present until

that date and further that an effort be made
to obtain an extension of the option on the
building previously considered until May 31st,
and that in connection with this campaign, we
endeavour to press the campaign as strenuously
as possible without *Gospel Witness* publicity
between now and March 31, and that the Finance Committee especially requests Mr. Carson
to give his whole time apart from that required
for services in Drummondville to canvassing the
Ottawa Valley constituency and other churches,
and that thereafter we endeavour to enlist the
services of such ministers as will be free to
help, and that the officers of the Committee
having this in charge are requested to do nothing that would be likely to jeopardize the appeal of Toronto Bapt. Sem. during the period
from now until March 31. [In other words, the
Gospel Witness, published by Jarvis Street Baptist Church and by far the most widely read
and influential publication in the Union, could
not be used for the appeal for Drummondville
because the Finance Committee did not want to
jeopardize the appeal for funds for TBS that
was then underway and would end on 31 March.
Apparently for the same reason Tom was urged
to canvass churches in the Ottawa Valley, three
hundred miles from Toronto.]

I was much puzzled by this action and also somewhat
distressed. Nevertheless, there seemed to me at the
time nothing against the Drummondville building campaign, and nothing against the particular building
we believed to be the one we should make every effort
to obtain. Otherwise no request would have been made
to try to get a further extension of the option, nor
would there have been any such urgent necessity "to
press the campaign as strenuously as possible without *Gospel Witness* publicity between now [Feb. 7] and
Mar. 31."

Therefore I took courage, and started to prepare
my campaign. My letter was ready to go out when I
received brother Hall's letter. In principle our letters agreed; yet there was no collusion between us
whatsoever. I certainly thought, as I stated in my

letter, that I had the backing of the Finance Committee. And the churches had begun to respond.

At first I felt reluctant to ask for an extension
of the option as requested by the Finance Committee.
However, following my illness, I went to see our real
estate agent, suggesting that for a further deposit
of $200 he might be able to obtain for us from the
vendor a three-week extension. He was unwilling to go
after it because, he said, it was practically useless
to expect much from the owner. A day or two later I
wrote the proprietor myself. At the same time I wired
Toronto asking an advance of $200 in case he should
agree.

It was then I received the worst shock of this campaign. Mr. Hall informed me in a letter from Noranda
dated March 15, 1948, "As things stand at the moment
we have no authority to forward any of the money, or
to expend any of it except as the Finance Committee directs. They did not so much as authorize the
purchase of the property under option." Exactly what
this meant we shall see.

In the meantime the vendor's counter-proposal came
in. He would agree to extend the option three weeks
if I should deposit another $1,000. That I did not
have, and was not then prepared to raise. I understood our agent's attitude now.

I spoke in a few places around Toronto from March
21st to March 24th. I tried to get another Finance
Committee meeting called to turn over the money that
had come in expressly for our property under option
at Drummondville, and that we might make arrangements
should we be short. More than $3,000 was already on
hand by Thursday morning, March 25th. But it was all
to no avail. Nothing was to be done until April 6th,
the date of the full Executive Board meeting—FIVE
DAYS AFTER EXPIRY DATE OF OUR OPTION. That last resolution of the Finance Committee was so drawn up as
to eliminate our property under option, the collateral from Union funds, the Snowdon Baptist Church as
trustees of the deeds, myself as the missionary, and—
whether they realized it or no—Drummondville, with
its 30,000 population, as a Union missionary field. I
am certain that the mover and seconder of the all-out
motion made the previous day did not realize its full
significance, for it was only "in view of the fact

that an earnest effort was to be put forth for the establishing of a work in Drummondville" that they were willing to rescind their motion.

When I came back from Toronto there remained but one course open for me. I went to the bank, and borrowed the $1,000 needed for the extension of the option, putting up less than half of that amount as collateral. With but two days remaining before the expiration of the option, I obtained an extension until April 21st. I think I had counted the cost. To me to let this go now was to throw away the greatest opportunity we have had for French-Canadian Roman Catholic evangelization. Montréal itself will only be greater when we have a centre of our own.

It is not my part to say what happened on the Board. I was not present. Only matters within my ken do I pass on. On April 6th the Board "appointed a second Committee so that the matter might be independently viewed through other eyes" (Board's letter). They were to meet with the Board again April 16th. This Committee was in Drummondville from Monday night April 12th to Wednesday morning April 14th. They saw none of our Christians there, in spite of the general statement of policy passed six days before. Then they returned with their report. The tenor of the Board's letter indicates that their report was preferred to that of the first Committee. They discouraged some of the members on the Board and made their hearts "melt." "Mr. Jennings moves that the Union make good to the friends in Drummondville the $500.00 paid for the option to March 31st re property on Mercure Blvd. (provided the option is not exercised), and that no property be purchased in Drummondville at the present time . . ." (Board's letter).

Strangely enough "The Chairman of [this] second Committee expressed the opinion that one needed really to be resident in the place for about three months properly to appraise the whole situation" (Board's letter, page 2). The first Committee had taken an appraisal of the situation over a period of several months; I myself had been spending two whole days a week over a period of six months in the work there; the believers had been there from six to twenty or more years. These were in complete agreement as to the necessity of obtaining a building, and the advisability of procuring such a suitable one as that on which we had taken out an option. Our churches responded gloriously, giving more than was required: the Board did not need to borrow one cent from their ordinary funds.

On April 17th I heard the news. With what seemed to me the clearest sort of evidence of God's leading and blessing on a project, if ever such were clear, with believers, funds and safeguards such as few beginnings have ever had, with an open door to an unevangelized city, among a numerous people whom I believed our Union had pledged itself to evangelize, with obstacles wonderfully overcome from our entry into this city last spring until this present date, with all that, our Board had voted not to go on.

The Board's letter states, "The action of the Board does not involve withdrawing from Drummondville, nor the abandonment or even diminution of our interest in French-Canadian evangelization." Yet after two or three months of waiting and praying and hoping and giving following years of discouragement, and knowing the evident success of the whole campaign among our churches, thus to be treated could scarcely suggest to these noble believers [in Drummondville]—and they are a noble band—other than a direct repudiation of themselves.

Thank God there is occasion for great gratitude to God. We are thankful for friends of this work on the Board; we are deeply grateful for our churches who have so heartily responded to this project. We are confident that many of them, if indeed not all, will dissociate themselves from the Board's action and see to it that their funds raised for this missionary enterprise shall be forwarded on to us. We are confident, too, that some at least, if not all, on the Board, when they understand the facts, will take similar action.

In any case, if you have already asked, or intend to ask that this money be forwarded, we ask you kindly to let us know of your action. We shall see to it that a receipt is forwarded to you from our Treasurer immediately upon receipt of your gift. Or, if it should be forwarded to us from the Union Office, we shall inform you immediately by letter. The Board's letter says clearly, "The Board would add

that, if any contributing church should be disposed
to ask that their contribution be returned for their
own disposition, the Board, of course, on request,
will be glad to return it." To all helpers in this
work it is our intention to forward a quarterly financial statement. We would provide things honest in
the sight of all men.

We are ready, by God's grace, to face the "strong
antipathy" "in a building . . . not fire proof" even
though it may be "hazardous," as per the Board's letter. For we dare to say with Joshua and Caleb, "The
land, which we passed through to search it, is an
exceedingly good land." The Lord has delighted in us
to "bring us into this land, and give it us; a land
which floweth with milk and honey." We ask you also
not to "fear . . . the people of the land, for they
are bread for us; their defence is departed from
them, and the Lord is with us; fear them not." We look
for the day, not far away, when the Lord from among
this people shall join the army of the Lord, and bear
testimony to His Name and to His great salvation.

May the Lord bless you all!

In His Name, and on behalf of the Drummondville
Christians, I am,

Yours for needy Québec,
T. D. M. Carson

P.S. Please forward all contributions either to
    Mr. Clarence Crook
    Box 197, St-Simon de Drummond, P.Q.
    or to myself at
    Box 473, Drummondville, P.Q.